MENORCA
A TOUR OF THE ISLAND

TRIANGLE BOOKS

Photography Biel Puig
Juanjo Pons
Ricard Pla
Jaume Serrat
David Arquimbau
Iñaki Relanzón
David Cardona
Laia Moreno
Miky Pons
Joan Mercadal
Kike Cardona
Oriol Aleu
Lluís Mas
Isolda Delgado
Isabel Martín

Text Joan Montserrat
Imma Planas (Information and suggestions)

Acknowledgements Lluís Plantalamor – Museu de Menorca
Aeroclub de Menorca

Grafic concept Joan Barjau
Anna Barjau

Illustrations Perico Pastor

Cartography Triangle Postals

Translation Steve Cedar

Printed by Litografia Rosés SA
Printed in Barcelona

Legally reg. Me-386-2017
ISBN 978-84-8478-776-1

G O I B CONSELLERIA CULTURA, PARTICIPACIÓ I ESPORTS / DIRECCIÓ GENERAL CULTURA

illenc Institut de la Llengua i la Cultura de les Illes Balears

CONSELL INSULAR DE MENORCA

MENORCA TALAIÒTICA Candidata Patrimoni Mundial Única al món

THE WHOLE COASTLINE FROM THE AIR
EXCURSIONS

An island of surprises

First-time visitors to the island usually say that it is unique, distinct and surprising. As luck would have it, Menorca still surprises its visitors. Its qualities are so many and so unexpected and disparate, that there is no one way of describing them, but even the briefest of visits will provide enough clues to the surprising nature of this very special island.

The second largest and most north-eastern of the Balearics, Menorca differs from the other islands in both climate and morphology. Throughout the course of history, successive changes of fortune have left their mark here, as have the diverse cultural influences of the many races who have occupied the island over the centuries. This turbulent past history has endowed Menorca with an original, distinctive character about which much has been written. The island not only offers a wealth of things to see, but also much food for thought and discussion.

Here, in the past, a high degree of independence existed between one township and another and, on occasions, this even degenerated into conflictive rivalry. Each centre of population sought to protect itself against loss of identity and living space by keeping its distance from its neighbours. In modern times, both the need for a more global territorial policy and improvements in transport and communications contributed to a rapprochement between them which put an end to the exaggerated insularity of these "islands" within an island.

In total contrast to this attitude, and perhaps as a result of the cultural and ethnic melting pot from which they descend, Menorcans have always been open and generous in their dealings with outsiders. Until quite recently, it was customary for front doors to be left unlocked at all times.

Peace and calm was a rule of life, the concept of cleanliness went beyond the insides of the houses to public spaces, the pace of activities followed the course of the sunlight...

It is not easy to maintain such a life-style when faced with the massive influx of tourists during the summer months, although the people of Menorca do strive to share it with their visitors and bear with good grace the difficulties that inevitably arise when the 90,000 inhabitants of the island find their numbers more than doubled.

If the service industries sometimes appear inadequate, it can only be attributed to the disproportionate demands made upon them. The island's resources must be administered

← Cala Macarelleta
↓ Binibequer Vell

The rural landscape has a dominant presence throughout the island. Es Castell

with care in order to ensure the continued survival of these privileged surroundings. However, in terms of quality of life, we should be aware that it is a luxury to be able to enjoy a setting that to a large extent has remained unharmed and loyal to the past. Today the inhabitants of the islands are very concerned about the protection of their environment. Until a few years ago, opposition to development projects in Menorca had been almost exclusively limited to minority groups who foresaw the irremediable damage that could result from indiscriminate urbanization. The concession by UNESCO in 1993 to name it a Biosphere Reserve attracted the more reluctant sectors to the idea of which, without a framework that defends and perpetuates this reality, it will be difficult to achieve harmonious development.

Another decisive step, along the same lines, has been the Llei d'Espais Naturals legislation which guarantees different levels of protection for almost the entire island. Between those classified as Àrees Naturals d'Especial Interès or Àrees Rurals d'Interès Paisatgístic, (local equivalent of Sites of Special Scientific Interest), altogether nineteen zones have been included which gives a clear indication of the extent of the natural wealth of the island along with the willingness and need to preserve them.

Geophysical features

In the south of the Golfe du Lion, Menorca is situated practically in the centre of the western Mediterranean, at a point almost equidistant between Marseille and Algiers in a north-south direction, and Castelló de la Plana on the Spanish mainland and Oristano on the isle of Sardinia in an east-west direction. The area of the island measures 701 km^2, the perimeter 290 km., and 48 km. is the longest distance between one end of the island and the other. The four most extreme points are, to the north Cap de Cavalleria; to the south Illa de l'Aire; to the east Cap de Sa Mola; and to the west, Cap de Bajolí. The distance between Ciutadella and Alcúdia, the closest point on the island of Mallorca, is 50 km.

An imaginary line drawn from Maó harbour, across the island, to Algaiarens would coincide with a natural division of the land which varies greatly between the

Cattle farming is the main agricultural activity

north and the south. Above this line we find the island's oldest terrain which, in part, pertains to the Paleozoic insular shelf and partly to the Triassic, Jurassic and Cretaceous eras. This combination results in an interesting contrast of colours and textures. It is an area of gently rolling hills, including El Toro (358 m.), S'Enclusa (274 m.), and Santa Àgueda (264 m.), the three highest points on the island.

A wide strip of Miocenic terrain overlapped the southernmost extreme of this area, forming a flat limestone surface. Later, torrents from the north eroded the soil and formed channels that remain today as the small, but deep, ravines or gorges that are characteristic of this part of the island. Here in the *migjorn*, the south of Menorca, the rock is calcareous and the sand white, whereas, in the *tramuntana*, or north, the rock is siliceous with traces of sandstone, slate and shale.

Water, light and wind

The animal and plant life of the island has adapted to the conditions of the subsoil and to the availability of water. The supply of drinking water has preoccupied Menorcans since the beginning of time, as is demonstrated by the prehistoric *cocons*, shallow niches excavated in the rock, and the cisterns and tanks of more recent times, thus showing that the collection of rain water has always been imperative as there are few natural sources. Principally, they are found in the south of the island, where the more permeable subsoil permits the formation of underground reserves.

Fortunately, the climate is very humid as compared to the rest of the archipelago. The visitor who has only seen Menorca during the dry summer months can hardly imagine the intense verdancy of the rest of the year. Except for years of generalized drought, the regularity of the rainfall and the abundant winter dews compensate for the summer dryness. Autumn, unknown here as a season, is replaced by the *primavera d'hivern*, or winter's spring. The mildness of the temperatures and the virtual absence of the deciduous trees that, in other latitudes, are the first indicators of the proximity of winter, add to the spring-like atmosphere that can be enjoyed here in October and November.

Mediterranean tortoise (*Testudo hermanni*), protected species

Another decisive characteristic of Menorca's climate is the constant presence of the wind. As there are no natural obstacles to stop it, the island is at the mercy of gusts from all directions. Those from the north are the most dominant and, among them, the fierce *tramuntana*, the strongest and most insistent, reaches speeds of between 35 and 90km. per hour. It has spectacular effects on the environment: bowing and reshaping trees and bushes in its path, hampering work on the land and at sea, and depositing harmful salt on crops and orchards. In compensation, the *tramuntana* brings with it an abundance of blue skies, clean atmosphere and brilliant sunshine...and the cows seem to thrive on the salty fodder.

Extreme temperatures are unknown here and records of significant snowfalls must be sought in the archives. In summer, the average temperature is 25ºC and in winter 12ºC and this temperate climate is an added attraction for the considerable number of retired people, British in the main, who choose Menorca as their residence.

EL TORO

At 358 metres above sea level, El Toro is the geographic centre of the island and a place of pilgrimage. Its location makes it a perfect vantage point from which the entire coastline of the island can be seen and, on clear days, Mallorca is visible on the horizon to the south-east. Once it was fortified to protect the islanders from the incursions of Berber pirates and today it is a spiritual refuge dedicated to Our Lady del Toro, patron saint of Menorca whose image, so legend has it, was discovered here by a friar following the signs passed onto him by a silver-hoofed bull. The monastery is inhabited today by Franciscan nuns.

←← "Red flies", (*Ophrys tenthredinifera*) one of the local orchids
← "Pig's ear", (*Dranunculus muscivorus*) another name befitting a curious flower

Flora and fauna

We have already mentioned the almost total absence of deciduous trees on the island. This is another consequence of the shortage of water which, in this instance, favours the growth of the evergreen varieties. Those which we could call "domestic" and which are common on the rest of the Balearics are on the decrease. Among these, the most common species are the carob, the almond, the fig and the wild olive, genetic predecessor of the olive tree. The prickly pear also abounds and is known to the Menorcans as the *figuera de moro* or Moor's fig, while the other is known as the *figuera de cristià,* the Christian fig.

For building material or firewood, the well-established wild olive or evergreen oak are used and they are the species that adapt best to the land and climate. In fact the wild olive and evergreen oak were and had to be the main island ecosystems, but in the woods in the centre and north there are two varieties of pine, as a precise result of their disappearance. There are sabines that grow close to the beaches and marshlands and there are also many coves surrounded by pine woods.

Other types of vegetation include the mastic bush, buckthorn, madronas, heather, myrtles, broom, oleander, bramble, juniper and more at ground level, liliaceas plants, such as the wild asparagus, arum plants

The mountain's name is derived from the pre-Romanesque noun tor, origin of the Catalan turó or hill. The Arabs called it Al Thor which had the same meaning. It is possible to walk to the top following a footpath on the north side.

The hill-top is somewhat cluttered with a profusion of communication aerials and antennas, and a rather perplexing memorial to the dead of the north-African war.

Common buzzard (*Buteo buteo*)

→
Common egret (*Egretta garzetta*)

→→
Egyptian vulture (*Neophron percnopterus*)

(such as the curious *bec de frare*, "friar's cowl") and some orchids, such as the so-called yellow and blue *mosques*, "fly" orchids. We can also see beach lilies in the dune areas, white and black stipa in deforested areas, or giant weeds in the wetter parts. Lichens cover the rocky spots and the wind-swept coastal area communities of dense and rounded spiny thicket, called *socarrells* (*Launaea cervicornis*).

The animal kingdom is made up of, on land, small mammals, reptiles, insects and many birds. Among the former feature martins, ferrets, weasels, rabbits, bats, some varieties of field mice and the shy hedgehog. Among the reptiles are the Mediterranean tortoise, wall lizards and some small and non-poisonous snakes. The population with most specific weight, however, is the winged kingdom. The fact that pairs of majestic red kites, and other birds of prey, are still a relatively frequent sight says much for the state of Menorca's wildlife, as their presence indicates the survival of many lesser species that form the lower echelons of the ecological pyramid.

Each of the different topographic areas of the island is host to many species of birds. In the gorges: turtledoves, wood pigeons and blackbirds. On the cliffsides and harbours: seagulls, storm petrel, shearwaters and cormorants. In the woods and on cultivated land: woodcocks, goldcrests, nightjars, flycatchers, partridges and quail. In more

***Sargantanes* (Lizards)**

There are as many subspecies of lizards as there are islets where they are found on them, and they are of great interest to naturalists and biologists. The populations from Illa de ses Sargantanes, Illa d'en Colom, Illa del Aire... in particular the latter, were decimated not long ago due to the demand for them from German terrariums, where they were wanted for their unusual black colour (although some say that they lose this trait shortly after being taken from their natural habitat). These endemic creatures, the result of centuries of isolation, can now be observed in situ thanks to the laws that protect them.

open spaces: larks, Thikla larks, corn bunting, hoopoes and crows. During the winter, robins and orphean warblers are to be seen, along with great flocks of thrush and starlings that stop in Menorca on their way south from the cold north and, during the summer, swallows, swifts, crag martins and bee-eaters arrive from North Africa.

Some parts of the island play such an important role in the migratory and reproductive cycles of these species that development projects in the vicinity have been prohibited. This is the case of Albufera d'Es Grau where, apart from an important resident colony, thousands of birds gather each year to breed. Ornithologist's can see mallards, coots, water rails, aquatic warblers, grebes, egrets, pochards and stone curlews in the waters, on the shores or among the reeds.

Various predatory and scavenger species can be observed all year round, although man's invasion of their nesting areas has led to the drastic reduction in the number of these larger birds. This is the case of the osprey, the booted eagle and even the red kite, but falcons, kestrels, hawks, Egyptian vultures, buzzards, marsh harriers and owls are still plentiful along with many types of small, insectivorous birds.

Red cows and black horses

The most common breed of cows seen in the fields –black and white over green– are examples of the Friesian breed. You will also see some herds of slightly woolly Charolais. However, attempts to recover the old reddish-coloured Menorcan cow, a rather intimidating character (if you come across them, it is best to keep your distance), are gradually bearing fruit.

And while the cows are red, the horses are jet black. With a magnificent appearance, the Menorcan horse deserves more than any other the title of noble beast. The leading star of the island's festivals, the sight of them is the finest representative, powerfully standing high on their back legs. Their manes and tails adorned with coloured ribbons, their nobleness is even more enhanced when they seem to allow the jockey the look of pride that they deserve.

Common octopus (*Octopus vulgaris*)

Caproig (redhead) is the name given to the large-scaled scorpion fish (Scorpaena scrofa) in these parts

The sea and its riches

The enjoyment of nature extends into the domains of sea, as is de rigueur on an island. Where the land ends, wave and tidal model a different landscape each step, each stroke. On land, attempting to walk the whole coastline has the interesting option of walking by the **Cami de Cavalls,** Horse Riding Track (1682), whose civilian and military use was common until the middle of last century. The Island Council, in collaboration with the municipalities, has managed to recover for the use of pedestrians, cyclists and mountain bike riders, but its size (about 110 miles) makes it inevitable to face it in multiple stages, section by section.

Another form of exploration is by sea. The custom of sailing round the island with overnight stops on the way, always a tradition among Menorcan families, many of whom possess recreational craft for this purpose, has also become popular with the visiting tourists. At the height of the season, the many boats to be seen in the coastal waters form a kind of pilgrimage.

The fact is that the Mediterranean continues to sculpt cliffs and caves, day in and day out, depositing pebbles and sandy areas, continually amazing us with its constant labour of transformation. Whoever has the chance to see this should not waste it.

Those visitors who do not have the opportunity to see the island by boat can console themselves relaxing and bathing on any of the magnificent beaches which also offer the possibility of contemplating the marine floor and its fauna. Diving enthusiasts can choose between rocky and sandy sea beds; the depths that are host to grouper and scorpion fish, and the carpet of posidonia, reservoir of life and breeding ground to many crustaceans and young fish. This underwater meadow, of great oxygen-generating potential, is of course, another symbol of conservationism, and must be protected against its greatest predator, mankind and his arts.

Through the abuse of these arts both the monk seal (*vell marí*) and the sea turtle have been eradicated from these waters, and although the number of species we could underline is large, we should realise that the fragility of this richness is real, and that any imbalance we cause will be in detriment to the environment.

History and society

Since time immemorial, Menorca has suffered the logical transormations of a conquered land: many peoples and cultures have succeeded one another in occupation, imposing their customs and leaving their indelible mark. Their many and varied influences coexist here, forming the interesting mosaic that is Menorca today, enriched by centuries of change and adaptation.

Before the Phoenicians called this island Nura (from the fires they saw on the coastline), peoples from the mainland of Spain and the oriental Mediterranean had settled here and developed cultures of which there are many remains to be seen. Traces of their cultures are still apparent today in the many prehistoric monuments scattered over the island. In fact, Menorca can boast of having the greatest concentration of them in the world. After centuries of neglect, much of this unique archaeological treasure has now been restored, and excavation work still in progress continually adds new discoveries. Recently, in caves in the Ciutadella and Es Migjorn areas, both human remains and others belonging to the *myotragus balearicus* (an extinct breed of goat) have been found along with bronze, ceramic and wooden objects, all in an excellent state of conservation.

The first recorded visitors were of a peaceable nature, first Phoenician and then Greek sailors seeking to expand their commercial activities across the Mediterranean. The Carthaginians, on the other hand, landed here with very different intentions. Led by Magón, Hannibal's brother, they forcefully recruited the legendary sling-shooters whose skill was to bring them fame in the Punic Wars.

The Greek name of Meloussa was changed to Minorica by the Romans when they conquered the island under Quintus Caecilius Metellus in 123 BC. They built roads and reinforced the settlements of Iammona (Ciutadella), Mago (Maó) and Sanisera (Sanitja), establishing the new province of Insulae Balearis. It appears that the natives of the island lived in harmony with the new occupiers until the 5th century AD and the arrival of the Vandals. Much has still to be discovered about the Roman occupation of the island as has become apparent following the new excavations being carried out on one third of the abovementioned sites in the port of Sanitja. The work includes underwater investigations in nearby waters .

For some time now, Christianity had become firmly established on the island. Bishop Severo's famous epistle of the year 417, describes travelling from Mago to Iammona with the aim of converting the city's Jewish

Pre-Talayotic funerary item dated around 1800-2000 BC. It forms part of the Vives Escudero collection

Reconstruction of a ceramic urn from the late Talayotic period. The fragments were found at the Trepucó excavation

Small bronze statue found in the Torre d'en Galmés excavation. It represents the healing god Imhotep and it is believed to date back to the late Talayotic period

colony. For this reason, when the Vandals, Arian in religion, appeared, there were bloody persecutions. Their stay, however, was brief. They were replaced by Byzantine expansion which coincided with a lapse of several centuries about which comparatively little is known.

Those years of probable misgovernment ended with the establishment of the flourishing Arab culture. In 903, under the new name of Minurka, the island came to depend on the Caliphate of Cordoba. In 1015 the Almohades were incorporated into the Taifa Kingdom of Dénia, who divided it into four districts and introduced irrigation systems and orchard cultivation. The population grew and different religions lived alongside each other in peace.

Roman coin, with the same value as a silver denarius, with the profile of the goddess Roma. It dates back to 146 BC, and was found in the Sanisera excavations

Small bronze bull found at Torralba d'en Salord taula. Probably a votive element, it dates from the 3rd or 4th century BC.

The Catalan conquest

The 13th century saw dramatic changes take place with the advance in Catalan-Aragonese weapons in the area comprising the western Mediterranean. Mallorca was taken by Jaume I and in 1232 Menorca declared feudal allegiance to him which was maintained until 1287 when the island was conquered by a confederate army led by Alfonso III of Aragon, who commanded an expedition made up of *"sicilians, mallorquins, catalans, aragonessos i almogàvers"*. The Moors were taken as slaves or sent home in return for ransom. Of the latter, many never arrived but were thrown overboard shortly after setting sail. Alfons III shared the reconquered land as booty among his knights and this led to a certain deterioration of the island's social and economic structure, something they tried to correct later on with the establishment of a parish system, the *universitats*, when the Treaty of Anagni had transferred sovereignty to the kingdom of Mallorca .

After a brief period of progress and improvement, and until the end of the Middle Ages, the history of Menorca can be summarised as a time of epidemics, poverty, decadence and confrontation between the ruling classes and the peasantry. Following this, the 16th century can only be described

This Gothic inscription, commemorating the conquest of the island by Alfons III, can be seen today in the Museu de Menorca. It comes from the Pont de na Gentil in Maó

For their similarity in terms of both style and subject matter, these oil paintings are attributed to the landscape painter Joan Font i Vidal (1811–1855), although only the second one, dated the "10th of October 1850" bears his signature

in even worse terms, as, during the negligent reigns of Carlos I and Felipe II, many tragedies took place. In 1535 a fleet led by the cruel Turk Barbarossa admiral of Sultan Solimán II, sacked the city of Maó, razed it to the ground and imprisoned the populace. Less than a quarter of a century later, in 1558, the Turk Mustafah Pilai attacked Ciutadella with even worse consequences. The capital also lost its heritage of historical documents.

The 17th century was as ill-fated as its predecessors. Epidemics of bubonic plague, the constant threat of pirate raids and the destruction of crops by swarms of locusts further undermined the peasantry while the nobility and the clergy grew stronger in the face of these adversities. The events of the 18th century and the change of sovereignty they brought were, therefore, beneficial. The century began with confrontations between followers of the Archduke of Austria, pretender to the Spanish throne, and those of Felipe of Bourbon. The outbreak of the War of Succession in 1706 plunged the island into a state of civil war. France sent troops to support the Bourbon cause, thus enabling Anglo-Dutch forces to disembark and take the island with hardly a shot fired. In 1712, the Treaty of Utrecht ceded the island of Menorca to the British Crown.

British and french domination

The British domination that lasted from 1708 to 1756 has been described by historians as the Golden Age of Menorca. If injustices were committed by some members of the governing body, they were rapidly rectified and Richard Kane, the first Governor, is remembered with praise. He introduced fodder farming, imported fresh breeding stock, built the road across the island that still bears his name, abolished the Inquisition, and built schools, along with many other improvements. Under his rule, only the interests of Ciutadella can said to have been prejudiced, on losing the status of capital in favour of Maó which benefited greatly from the consequent increase in commercial activity. This domination ended in 1756, when the Duke of Richelieu, with a contingent of twenty thousand French troops, disembarked in Ciutadella and the British withdrew on friendly terms. For the next seven years, until 1763, Menorca was

ruled by the French who undertook a policy of peaceful coexistence with the islanders. During this time, the Governor, Count of Lannion, reinstated some of Ciutadella's lost status and founded the village of Sant Lluís in honour of King Louis. When the Treaty of Paris returned Menorca to the British Crown, the booty they took with them did not go much beyond the recipe for *mayonnaise*.

During this second domination, the British were not as benevolent as they had been in the past. A number of Menorcans, owing to the conditions of extreme poverty and hunger that now prevailed, emigrated to Florida in search of better fortune and others became privateers. The only notable work carried out by them was the demolition of the suburb of Sant Felip and the transfer of its inhabitants to Georgetown, today Es Castell. After nineteen years of bad government and injustice, in 1782, a Franco-Spanish fleet, under the orders of the Duke of Crillon, re-conquered the island under Spanish sovereignty and one of the first measures adopted was the blowing-up of the mythical castle of Sant Felip.

In 1798 the British returned for the last time, staying until 1802 when Menorca was finally returned to the Spanish Crown after seventy-two years of foreign occupation. Despite the good government of the Count of Cifuentes, Carlos III's representative on the island, the Spanish administration brought with it the seal of totalitarianism with a consequent loss of civil liberties, and, during the reigns of Carlos IV and Fernando VII, decadence and corruption prevailed throughout society. Once again, emigration was the only solution for many Menorcans who now ventured to Algiers and other north-African cities.

Not until the middle of the 19th century did industrialisation permit a relative economic recovery.

Recent history

This industrialisation brought with it the beginnings of labour movements which, in turn, instigated many social changes. For example, a general strike was held in protest against the war in Morocco and the workers of the shoemaking industry formed a federation under the leadership of the anarchist Joan Mir i Mir. The collapse of the

First Republic and the return of the Bourbon Monarchy, supported by the landowning aristocracy, strengthened the position of the old ruling classes. The parliamentary elections of 1879 were won by the Conservatives in the Balearics, their member for Menorca being the Duke of Almenara Alta.

With the ascension to the throne of Alfonso XIII in 1902, the whole Spanish political system of the Restoration entered into a period of crisis and both Liberals and Conservatives failed in their attempts at innovation. In Menorca, only the Conservatives carried any weight within Monarchist circles, but the Republican Party was strongly supported and in several legislations represented the island at Parliament. Proof of the Menorcans' truly democratic disposition at that time can be found in their lack of support for neither the candidatures presented by Joan March in Mallorca and Pere Matutes in Eivissa, nor the reactionary dictatorship of Primo de Rivera. At the local elections of 1931, the results of which led to

Anonymous painting, dated 1835, in which the activities of Maó harbour are illustrated in great detail. The warehouses in the foreground stand at the foot of the hill that connected the quayside with what is now the Miranda Square. Social classes such as merchants and clergy are represented, as are the different trades of the time: boatbuilders, peasants, fishermen, dockers, gin distillers, etc.

the proclamation of the Second Republic, the seat for Menorca was won by the Front Únic Antimonàrquic, made up of socialists and republicans.

The Spanish Civil War had very dramatic effects on Menorcan society. Following the Nationalist insurrection that gave rise to the outbreak of the Spanish Civil War, the military commander declared the island's allegiance to the Francoist rebellion. However, the very next day, 20th July 1936, a combined force of civilians and non-commissioned officers rose against the insurgent armed forces and, at the cost of great loss of life, won Menorca back for the Republic.

The island resisted until the end of the war in February 1939 and was, in fact, the last position in Spain to fall to the Nationalist troops. The bloody reprisals perpetrated in retaliation form one of the most traumatic chapters of Menorcan history.

The social and economic consequences of nearly forty years of dictatorship are too far-reaching and complex to be dealt with here

Oil painting on canvas, dated and signed B. Pax 1859, showing the Industrial Mahonesa factory, opened in 1856 in Cala Figuera

in detail. The one-party system, strengthened by a powerful bureaucracy, generated political apathy among the populace and, until the 1950s, there was no apparent sign of unrest at any social level. The latter end of the 1960s, a time of prosperity for the island, witnessed the first, albeit clandestine, indications of a desire for the revival of democracy. They were to remain repressed until the 1970s and the flood of events that changed the course of Spanish history: the death of the dictator and restoration of the monarchy in King Juan Carlos I (November 1975), the reform process that led to the first democratic elections since the Second Republic (June 1977), and the enactment by the King of the new Constitution (December 1978), supported by the majority of political parties.

Later, on the 17th of February 1982, Parliament accepted the Estatut d'Autonomía de les Illes Balears which allows a degree of home rule for the islands under the Consells Insulars, or island councils.

The economy

The basis of the island's current economic profile must be sought in the first shoe factories that were set up in Ciutadella around the year 1850. The process from craftsmen's industry to full industrialisation with the use of machinery marked the start of a pre-capitalist era in which Menorcan produce was successfully promoted abroad. Commerce with both the continent and the Spanish colonies brought notable progress and prosperity to the island and gave rise to the creation of other subsidiary activities.

Industries were created and banks were opened. In 1856 the Industrial Mahonesa opened the island's pioneer textile and cotton-spinning factory in Cala Figuera, in the port of Maó, and the following years were a time of prosperity during which many businesses and industries were set up. The loss of the Cuban market in 1898 plunged the shoemaking industry into a severe recession which lasted until the First World War. At the same time, however, by 1911 three thousand people were employed in the manufacture of silver purses. This industry, started at the beginning of the 20th century and very important until 1925, is considered to be the precursor of the present-day costume-jewellery industry.

After 1870, the extensive cultivation of cattle fodder converted dairy farming into the principal agricultural activity with the consequent increase in meat and milk production, the latter being made into cheese.

Tourism, as an industry, arrived in Menorca between the end of the 1950s and the beginning of the 1960s, but its advance was far slower than in Mallorca or Eivissa due to the fact that, here, it was considered an alternative source of income rather than the mainstay of the economy. Even so, by 1975 it was important enough to be considered as one of the three chief economic supports, the others being arable and dairy farming, and the costume-jewellery and shoemaking industries.

This balance was upset by a series of events, such as Spain's entry into the E.C. in 1986 which severely affected the dairy farming industry, and the strong competition presented to the costume-jewellery and footwear sectors by Asian manufacturers whose labour and raw material costs cannot be rivalled here. Above all else, one should take into account the high cost of commercial viability in terms of the import of raw materials for the industrial process not available here. The costs of isolation seem insuperable, and it is yet to be seen how the island's industries will deal with the challenges to be faced in this millennium.

Footwear and avarques

A census carried out in 1782 (when Menorca was once again under Spanish rule) indicated that 281 islanders were shoemakers by trade. Their customers were members of the aristocracy and military officers, and the first steps were being taken to establish an export trade. Since those days, this industry has known times of great prosperity but also important setbacks and recessions such as the loss of the Cuban market at the turn of the century. Thanks to the skill and professionalism of the craftsmen of Alaior and Ciutadella, the prestige of Menorcan footwear prevails today.

As competition intensified from other sources with lower production costs, the industry here was obliged to move up into the market of fashion-design. Nevertheless, one of the most successful lines are the peasant sandals or avarques, comprised of two pieces of cowhide attached to a pneumatic sole, guaranteeing thousands of kilometres of walking and well ventilated feet. They are such an intrinsic symbol of Menorcan summertime that miniature china copies are sold as souvenirs.

Prehistoric monuments

Following the stone route that marks out these vestiges is one of the best distractions for the curious traveller, although an exhaustive visit to so many archaeological sites requires a lot of time. The simplest route we can suggest is the South-eastern Area car tour (see page 140) and the indications at the end of the Around Ciutadella tour (see page 138). In any case, at least do not miss the chance to see the first talayot or *taula* that you pass on the way. The oldest remains (megalithic tombs, underground caves and navetas) have been dated by experts at around 2000 BC, but the most notable examples date from what is known as the Talayotic era, from around 1400 BC to the Roman invasion of the island in the last century BC. During this time, the structural conception, and even some of the materials used, changed considerably, to a certain extent as a result of increased contact with the outside world. Successive stages of this process are quite patent in some cases, the last recognisable influence being Punic, coincid-

Naveta des Tudons, the most outstanding burial chamber. In the picture at the top of the page, the settlement of Talatí de Dalt

Burial caves of Cala Morell

ing with the foundation of Mago, Iammona and Sanisera. These settlements were still inhabited by the native population during the Roman occupation. The monuments that date from the Talayotic era are easily recognizable and are classified as: burial caves, burial *navetes*, naviforms, talayots, walled enclosures and taules.

Monuments from other historical periods to be found on the island are the early-Christian basilicas built in the period of North African influence (the Vandal kingdom of Carthage), and later on under Byzantine domain (Oriental Roman Empire). The first of these, that of **Son Bou**, dating from the 5th century, has a beautiful design and a baptismal font dug out from a stone. In contrast, at **Es Fornàs** there is another basilica dated the 6th century BC, with a semi-spherical baptismal font and superb floor mosaics (outstanding are those of a peacock and a lion, and another on the **Illa del Rei** whose mosaics have been moved to the Museu de Menorca. Two more are to be found at **Cap d'es Port de Fornells** and on the **Illa d'en Colom**, with a star-shaped baptismal font the latter currently undergoing excavation work.

Burial caves

The most interesting of their kind are to be found at **Calescoves**, on the south coast a few kilometres from Sant Climent, where there are nearly one hundred on the cliff face, giving it an impressive appearance. There are more at **Caparrot de Forma** (near Es Canutells), at **Son Bou** (beneath a fortified wall on the cliff) and at **Cala Morell** on the north coast. All these burial sites date from the 9th and 8th centuries BC, but seem to have been in use well into the Roman era.

Burial *navetes*

The name *naveta* (little boat) is derived from their appearance, resembling that of an inverted hull. The oldest, dating from pre-Talayotic times, are oval or circular in shape, but their construction evolved towards more elongated forms, for example, the most famous one of all, **Naveta des Tudons**, dated around 1400 BC. A tiny doorway gives access to the interior which is comprised of an anteroom or entrance hall and one or two superimposed chambers. These constructions, of purely funerary use, are the oldest in Europe of their kind and can be found at **Biniac**, **Llumena**, **Binimaimut**, **Rafal Rubí** and **Son Morell**.

Talaiot de Torelló, close to the airport

Talaiots

Talayots are situated on rises in the ground or hillocks, from where other talayots are usually visible at a distance. This fact has led to the supposition that they were used as defence towers or lookout points (*talaies* in Catalan), hence their name. However, remains have been found in small chambers inside these truncated cones which suggest that they were used as burial places. Their solid appearance is due to the large blocks placed in rows of a smaller perimeter as it reaches the top. Below these there are other smaller stones that make up the false dome. The most notable ones are: **Talatí**, of trapezoidal flat stones, **Trepucó**, the biggest; those of **Torelló** and **Cornia** (all the above around Maó) and those of **Torrellafuda** and **Montefí**, in Ciutadella.

Taules of Talatí de Dalt and Torre Trencada (in the silhouetted image)

Taules

These are the most exceptional of all the Talayotic monuments and are unique to Menorca, whereas constructions similar to talayots are to be found elsewhere. They comprise of two huge blocks of limestone and owe their name *taules* (tables in Catalan) to their T-shaped form. Their most notable characteristic is their size: the *taula* at Torralba d'en Salord, which is imbedded two metres in the ground, weighs approximately 25 tons. They are surrounded by a series of niches, forming a horse-shoe shaped precinct, which were probably used for depositing offerings to the deity. The space it occupies in the centre of the settlement lends weight to the idea that it was a kind of sanctuary. Opinions vary as to the purpose of this taula, some stating it is a fertility symbol in the form of the head and horns of a bull... The most well-known are at **Trepucó, Torre Trencada and Talatí de Dalt** (both with support frames), **Torre Llafuda, Torre Llisà Vell**, **Torre d'en Gaumés** and **Binimaimut**.

Rural architecture

The rural architecture of Menorca, so different from that of Mallorca, Eivissa or other parts of the Mediterranean, forms an integral part of the landscape and, as such, has a significance that rises above and beyond merely practical considerations.

The whiteness of the farmhouses and hamlets scattered across the countryside is one of the island's most characteristic images. More than half a century ago, the writer Josep Pla stressed this typical sight by pointing out, "The Menorcans love to frenetically whitewash their houses". The task of whitewashing was an activity that was usually done by the women, and ensured that the walls were clean and protected, without which the limestone with which they are built would be eaten away by sun, rain and wind. This stone, the *marès*, and *ullastre*, the wood from the wild olive tree, were the only raw building materials to be found on the island. Easily cut into ashlars, or building blocks, marès was readily available, either at the building site itself, or from any of the many quarries. Some of these are still operating today and are interesting spots to visit.

The basic configuration of Menorcan rural architecture was determined by the limited range of available raw materials and the prevailing climate. Houses were always built facing south, with a minimum of doors and windows on the north side to exclude the cold *tramuntana* wind. The sun heats the porches during the winter months and rainwater is collected by a curious system of gutters made from Moorish-style roof tiles that canalise it down from the roof to the cistern or water tank. All these elements make the Menorcan farmhouse a clear example of man's adjustment to the means at his disposal. The farmer is still the master of the house, although sometimes they are shared with the landowner's family, whose presence is only noticeable from the new rooms that go beyond practical use, stairways and even the odd neo-classical façade.

Another characteristic of the countryside are the endless dry-stone walls that, when seen from the air, appear as an enormous crisscross network. Their purpose is to divide up the *llocs* or farmsteads into individual *tanques* or fields for crop rotation. At the same time, their construction cleared the fields of stones and prevents the sparse topsoil from being blown away by the strong winds. Some of these stones were used to construct protective walls around tree trunks. True craftsmen, the few remaining *paredadors*, the wall builders, still work in the same ancestral way building a double wall which is then filled in with rubble. To make them easier to climb, a few stones are left protruding up both sides to form rudimentary steps known as *botadors*. The wooden gates, often made of twisted olive tree wood, another example of local craftsmanship, prevent cattle and sheep from straying and should always be left as they are found.

Porxada of the Torre d'en Quart estate in Ciutadella

→
Sant Joan de Missa

→→
Diverse examples of rural architecture

QUARRIES

The association between Menorca and stone, whether in its natural state or manipulated by man, is inevitable. The stone ties and supports the island's scenery wherever you look. When building styles moved away from the use of rudimentary, crude stone towards the use of limestone ashlars, these were invariably obtained from the sites themselves. Later, the increasing demand gave rise to the construction of quarries where thousands of tons of raw material were hewed, by hand, in regular shaped blocks.

Times have changed, and the introduction of new elements has caused the quarries to fall into disuse. The fact is, however, that they are a monument to man's efforts to live from the environment around him, and to a trade in danger of extinction. They are also curiosities for the visitor open to new experiences, and a spectacular space for concerts and recitals, as has been proved by Líthica, the association founded with the sole aim of protecting them.

Festivals

Uncontrolled merriment, crowds, feverish excitement and enthusiasm that spread to even the most reluctant... the festivals of Menorca have to be seen to be believed. They are a veritable explosion of energy, with the leading part played by the fantastic horses. Throughout the summer, each town celebrates in turn its own local *festes*, culminating in the festival of Maó, on the 7th and 8th of September. The first and most famous of these events is held in Ciutadella in honour of St. John the Baptist. The Festes de Sant Joan begin on the Sunday prior to June 24th, *Diumenge des Be*, when a beautiful sheep is paraded around the streets of the city, and reach their climax on the night before St. John's day. The official acts are based on medieval traditions, safeguarded by the *Junta de Caixers*, committee which represents the different historical social classes, peasantry, nobility and clergy, all of which are symbolically represented in the processions. This association, under whose care was the hermitage of Sant Joan, form a procession that precedes a *fabioler*, who on the back of a donkey, is in charge of marking the rhythm with the sound of his flageolet. From the moment when the cavalcade of horsemen enters into Es Born, the pace becomes vibrant. Spiralling turns, races, a ceremonial rite led by the chanting and getting louder and louder. You have to run, drink gin and get closer to the horse when the typical shouting and clapping raises the mounts. Its ancient origin is clearly expressed in the costumes, in the flag with the cross of the knights of Malta and the equestrian skills with which the horsemen handle their mounts (*ensortillades, ses carotes, córrer abraçats*), but the people experience it as a timeless event: you have to really experience it close up, once every summer...

←
Old engravings showing two of the symbols of the Festes de Sant Joan

↑
Gegants in the Festes de Gràcia in Maó

→
On the next page, caixers and horses in full action in the streets of Ciutadella

From east to west

Maó

The façades of the oldest buildings in Maó are again being painted the pale sienna colour that had been customary until, in an attempt to live up to the slogan "Menorca, the blue and white island", an over-zealous mayor ordered them all to be whitewashed. Much restoration and conservation has been carried out and the doorknobs are polished with more energy than ever. Behind the English-style sash windows hang lace curtains. In the early morning, before the first onslaught of traffic, it is easy to imagine the aspect the town presented at the height of its prosperity in the 18th century, and the liberal and cultured society that developed here.

Clustered high on the cliff, the old part of the city overlooks the harbour. The views from the stately houses on Carrer Isabel II, among which features the Military Command building, are particularly splendid as befits their opulent interiors and the ample proportions of their frontages. At one end of this street is the **convent of Sant Francesc**, the first built in Maó in 1719. The Baroque cloister houses the collections of the **Museu de Menorca**. In a very interesting setting, the pieces show the social and cultural development of the island from prehistoric times through to today.

At the opposite end of Isabel II in Pla de sa Parròquia (or Pla de Santa Maria) we find the church of the same name, the neo-classical **Town Hall**, with the clock given to the city by Governor Kane, and the building known as **Principal de Guàrdia**, painted red as befits English taste. The Town Hall houses a collection of portraits of famous historical figures, notably that of the Count of Lannion by Giuseppe Chiesa and the Count of Cifuentes by Pascual Calbó.

The **church of Santa Maria** is home to one of the city's treasures: the magnificent organ of 3210 pipes, 51 stops and 4 keyboards built by the German maestros Otter and Kirburz. The quality of its register delights those who attend the concerts given regularly by internationally renowned musicians who consider it a privilege to perform here. Behind Santa Maria, built in the reign of Alfons III, a statue of this king stands in the centre of the Plaça de la Conquesta, also site of the **Can Mercadal palace** and today the public library. One corner of the square

The city of Maó was founded and has grown due to the magnificent port that it overlooks from its stone throne

opens on to the viewpoint which overlooks the **Costa de Ses Voltes**, a landscaped stairway leading down to the port, one of the key images first perceived by visitors arriving by boat. At its foot is the area of the port known as **Baixamar**, today a nucleus of bars and restaurants and centre of the city's nightlife, particularly in the summer.

Traces of the commercial activity that used to be the main characteristic of the harbour can still be found in the remaining old buildings, once the workshops of the *mestres d'aixa*, or artisan boatbuilders. Their skills are still renowned today and can be appreciated in the custom-built *llaüts*. These vessels are no longer used solely as fishing boats, but have become the ideal recreational craft for the many people who explore the island's coastline during the summer months. Indeed, the whole aspect of the harbour has changed as a result of the growing popularity of nautical sports, one more aspect of the influence of tourism. Nowadays, hardly anyone remembers when merchant ships docked here to unload grain for grinding in Menorcan mills, en route to their final destination on the mainland of Spain (a law prohibited the stop-offs and the subsidiary industry to the benefit of Castile) or the presence of fleets flying all kinds of flags. Today, the craft found alongside the Club Marítim are modern, luxurious yachts, and more facilities for mooring and wintering are planned for the future.

Let's return, however, to the starting point of our descent down to the waterfront, the Costa de Ses Voltes. This is where the **fish market** is to be found and, a little further on, the meat, fruit and vegetable market, situated in what was once **the cloister** and ground floor cells of the convent adjoined to the **Carme church**. The market itself is well worth visiting for the originality of its setting and it is also a short cut through to Plaça Miranda, another excellent viewpoint over the harbour. From here, via Plaça del Príncep, we return to the pedestrian zone of **S'Arravaleta** and **Carrer Nou**, and the **Hannover** and **Deià** rises, with the small square of **Colón** in the centre. This is the commercial centre of the town and the number and nature of passers-by are an indication, in summer, of the success of the tourist season, and in winter a mirror of Menorcan society.

Mahon–Menorca cheese

Even though it is produced all over the island, Menorcan cheese is referred to as Maó as its commercialization has always been based in the capital. It also therefore comes under the Denomination of Origin label, awarded in 1985. Since the 1960s, the cheese produced on the island can be calculated in millions of kilos per year. Its quality was already being praised in medieval chronicles that tell of the predilection of the Catalan kings for this variety.

It is a half-fat cheese, made from full cow's milk to which a maximum permitted 5% of ewe's milk may be added. The cheeses are square in shape with rounded edges and, when handmade in the traditional way, bear characteristic marks caused by the white linen cloth in which the milk, once curdled, is wrapped. The whey is drained out manually and the bundle left under weights for twenty-four hours. Then it is submerged in salt water for two days before the drying process is started. According to the degree of maturity, it is sold as *tendre* (soft), *semicurat* (mild), *curat* (mature) or *vell* (vintage). It is delicious in any form, a delight appreciated by the most demanding palates.

Plaça del Carme in Maó. In the background the church of Santa María

Modernist façade of Casa Mir

The Cuesta Deià leads up to the **Teatre Principal**, inaugurated as an opera-house in 1829 and, as such, older than the Liceu of Barcelona. The Montcada house on the corner of Carrer del Bastió and Carrer Hannover has a striking modernist *boinder* (the name is a local evolution of the English bow window, an element often adopted here instead of typically Mediterranean balconies for climatic reasons. Further along, in Plaça Bastió, we reencounter the remains of the medieval city walls, the **Arc de Sant Roc** which leads to S'Arraval, the gateway that separated what were once the fortified city and the suburbs.

Another important central street is Dr. Orfila (or **Carrer de ses Moreres**), into which both Carrer Cifuentes and Cós de Gràcia converge from opposite sides. Following Es Cós, we arrive at the cemetery and shrine of Our Lady of Grace, patron saint of the city. The old orthodox temple of Sant Nicolau stands on the corner of Carrer Ramon y Cajal which leads, in turn, to the **Es Freginal** park, once a place of communal market-gardening. The scientific and literary **Athenaeum**, home of an important collection of fossils and algae and site of many cultural activities, stands in Carrer Conde de Cifuentes and, behind it, **S'Esplanada**, the main square of the modern city.

Bordered by the barracks built during the first British domination, the construction of an underground car park altered, yet again, the configuration of the old parade ground. Here people of all ages gather to pass the time of day and a handicraft and antique market is held twice a week. It is also the point of departure of the main roads that lead to Sant Lluís, Ciutadella and Sant Climent, the latter linked with the industrial estate and the airport, therefore also being an arrival point.

The best example of the non-stop growth of the city is a new district in Malbúger, where single-family homes alternate with large buildings, such as the home of the Consell Insular and the new general hospital.

The mooring quay of Cales Fonts, in Es Castell, is a very lively spot on summer nights

The old flour mill of Sant Lluís now exhibits tools traditionally used in farming

Es Castell

After the disappearance of the castle of Sant Felip and the surrounding suburb, in 1877 the English decided to build this town, which they called Georgetown. At the end of their occupation, Spanish troops changed its name to Villacarlos after King Carlos III of Spain, which it held until the official renaming of **Es Castell**, in reference to the old fortress. With the repositioning, the town gained in terms of urban development but it never lost its military aspect, as is still apparent in the barracks that surround **S'Esplanada**, the main square, alongside the colonial-style Town Hall. Inside the neo-classical church of Roser there is an interesting stone altarpiece that once belonged in the castle chapel.

Cales Fonts, down on the waterfront, was once the site of fishermen's boathouses but, over the years, has been transformed into lively centre of bars and restaurants. From here, sightseeing trips by boat can be taken around Maó harbour and over to **Llatzaret**. This fortified precinct only became an island in 1900 when the Alfons XII canal was constructed, and it served as a quarantine centre in the 18th and 19th centuries. Today it is used as a congress centre and visits, previously concerted, during the summer months. There is a small museum of medical instruments and other curiosities in one of the buildings.

Sant Lluís

Sant Lluís was founded at the end of the 18th century during the French occupation. They layout of its streets was planned by the Count of Lannion, as was the building of some of the outlying hamlets. In those days, their function was purely rural, but of late they have become residential areas. However, thanks to local legislation, their original outward appearance has been conserved.

In the town itself, the major landmarks are the governor's house and the church dedicated to the patron saint, Sant Louis, King of France. Several old windmills still stand, and one, the Molí de Dalt, has been converted into an interesting ethnological museum.

The coastline around Sant Lluís abounds

The church of Santa Eulària overlooks the original centre of Alaior

The port of Fornells is the "world capital" of the lobster stew

in coves, beaches and urbanizations: **S'Algar, Alcalfar, Punta Prima, Binisafúller** and **Binibèquer** all bear witness to the growth of the tourist industry with pretty white houses and clear waters. If visiting the town the route around the surrounding country houses should not be missed (Torret, S'Ullastrar...), which can be extended as far as the nearby centre of **Llucmassanes**, part of Maó.

Alaior

In 1304, King Jaume II of Mallorca founded what we know today as Alaior on the site of a farmstead named Ihalor. It is sometimes called the island's third capital on account of its historical role as mediator between Maó and Ciutadella and the independence afforded it by a balanced economy based on farming, tourism and light industry, in particular the footwear and cheese maturing factories (easily locatable due to the smell). **Son Bou, Sant Jaume** and **Cala en Porter** are the main tourist centres of the area.

The most notable buildings are **Casa Salord** and the one which now houses the **Town Hall**, and the **church of Santa Eulària** (rebuilt in Baroque style after damage by a tornado at the end of the 17th century). The cloister of the church of **Sant Dídac**, with a Plateresque doorway, now popularly known as **Pati de Sa Lluna**, has undergone a major transformation over the years and is now used for social andcultural purposes. Outside the town, the visitor may be surprised to see a number of houses of intriguing names and architectural styles that seem out of place in the Menorcan countryside.

Es Mercadal occupies the central part of the island

They were built by local people of past generations who ventured overseas during the economic recessions that afflicted the island and evoke memories of the exotic lands they visited.

Es Mercadal and Fornells

At the geographical heart of the island, at the foot of **El Toro**, Es Mercadal owes its name to the privilege bestowed by King Jaume II to Catalan colonials, authorizing them to hold a market here every Thursday of the year. This custom prevails today in a handicraft market also held on Tuesday and Saturday afternoons. The majority of the population is still employed on the many outlying farms. However, in neighour- ing **Fornells** and the nearby urbanizations, the local people both experience and make a living from the tourist industry and all that it involves. The island's only golf course is to be found near here at **Son Parc**.

The parish **church of Sant Martí** in Es Mercadal is a renaissance building with some later additions dating from 1807. Also worth seeing is the cistern, the *aljub* **d'en Kane**, built under British patronage by Pere Carreras in 1735. Regarding other questions, if we say that Fornells is an absolute must for whoever is a fan of lobster dishes, then Es Mercadal is a recent centre of "pilgrimage" for lovers of good food. With the idea of new flavours in mind, the most successful restaurants today are those offering typical dishes and products with a modern touch. Nor should we forget that here we find the **Centro Artesanal de Menorca** (Artisan Center of Menorca). Homemade sweets and confectionery and *avarques*, typical sandals, are two attractions for visitors.

Protected by the old church, the oldest houses of Ferreries resist the changes that enlarge the town

A street in Es Migjorn that shows in colours the desire in Menorca to place itself between the earth and the sky

Ferreries

Ferreries exemplifies the transformation that has taken place on the island since the beginning of tourist-orientated development in the 1960s. The shoe, costume jewellery and furniture-making industries employ a sector of the population previously dedicated to agriculture, and dairy farming has taken over from arable farming as the major rural activity. Building, commerce and service industries complete the rest of the town's economic profile. Opinions are divided over the origins of the name Ferreries, some opting for the existence of a nearby monastery of friars, *fraria*, and others for the idea that it was founded by a blacksmith, *ferrer*. What is for certain is that the town was established by King Jaume II of Mallorca, in the 14th century, who built the **church of Sant Bartomeu** which presides over the centre of the old town. However, the remodelled Plaça d'Espanya is the centre of activity today and on Saturdays hosts a handicraft and local produce market.

In the neighbouring area, places of interest include the **Algendar gorge**, **Cala Galdana** and **Santa Àgueda** (264m.) where the ruins of a 13th-century Moorish fortification still stand.

Es Migjorn

Es Migjorn became a municipality in its own right in 1989, (previously it was dependant on Es Mercadal), but its origins must be sought two centuries before during the second British occupation. Until then, the local farmers had to take their produce to Ferreries to be sold, but the construction of the **church of Sant Cristòfol** and surrounding dwellings offered them alternative trading opportunities. There is a small museum dedicated to Doctor Camps, a reputed expert in folklore who published his work under the pseudonym of **Francesc d'Albranca**.

Ciutadella

Ciutadella... is **Ciutadella**. However much we try and compare it to other cities or towns of similar evolution, a series of characteristics combine here to create a special atmosphere, an intangible difference. Its inhabitants are aware of this and maintain it with pride, as if in retaliation for the loss of their city's status as island capital. The city, however,

In summer, the port of Ciutadella plays host to most of the activities, both day and night

despite having experienced uncontrolled growth in recent years, preserves the charm that has always seduced its visitors, particularly in the old quarter.

Of the old city walls, only two bastions have survived the course of history: **Es Born** on top of which the **Town Hall** was built and **Sa Font**, at the point where a stream once emerged into the harbour. It is, however, easy to imagine the totality of the original form of the walls as they have been replaced by three consecutive avenues: **Constitució**, **Jaume I**, and **Capità Negrete**, known collectively as **Sa Contramurada**. The arch that they form, marking the limits of the old city, leads to the Plaça Alfons III where the **Porta de Maó** gateway once was. The final stretch of the main road is still called **Camí de Maó**, and is now an exclusively pedestrian zone when it crosses the square. On one of its corners stands the **Es Comte** windmill, now adapted to new uses.

Continuing along the Camí de Maó, we arrive at **Sa Plaça Nova**, occupied as before by the chairs and tables of the nearby bars. We then enter Carrer José Maria Quadrado, or **Ses Voltes**, one of the most characteristic streets. Its narrow pavement is widened by the vaulted arcade of the houses that flank it, a harmonious succession of arches only broken by the slight widening of **Sa Plaça Vella**, overlooked by one of the city's most emblematic symbols, on top of a sober column, the tiny *Be de Sant Joan* (Lamb of St. John), work of the local artist Maties Quetglas. Although the ground floors of the buildings in this street are today clothes shops, sweet shops and other outlets, it has lost none of its medieval charm, and ends precisely in the Plaça de la Catedral.

The **Santa Maria cathedral** does not stand out from its surroundings in terms of height, but the density of the setting enhances its forceful aspect. Built in Catalan Gothic style in the 14th century, it stands on the site of a Moslem mosque that had already been converted to Christianity after the arrival of Alfons III. It has a single large nave that has been repaired and rebuilt so many times that elements of various architectural styles are to be found, such as the Baroque **chapel of Ses Ànimes** and the neoclassical main façade. Historical events of all kinds have left their mark here, notably in 1558, *l'any de*

Pla de Sant Joan, in the port outlet, is the main stage for the festivals

Another typical image of Ciutadella: Ses Voltes

sa desgràcia (the year of misfortune), when the cathedral was razed to the ground during ferocious Turkish reprisals. Recently, the **Portal de la Llum** has been restored and several gargoyles replaced.

Before proceeding on to **Es Born** or main square, it is well worth strolling around the adjoining back streets. Facing the cathedral is the **Palau Olives** and behind it, attached, is the **Episcopal Palace**. A little further on, in Carrer Sant Sebastià, is the the **Palau Squella**. In Carrer Santa Clara, the **Palau Lluriach**, home of Menorca's oldest titled family, the Barons de Lluriach, and the **Convent of Santa Clara** whose tales of martyrs, arson and abductions form an intrinsic part of Ciutadella's history.

Carrer del Roser, on the other side of the **Pla de la Seu**, leads us to the church of Our Lady of the Rosary (**del Roser**) with its ornately decorated Baroque doorway, site of the municipal art gallery. In Carrer Bisbe Vila, one of the **Saura palaces**, occupied today by a bank, and beside it the Renaissance Augustinian **convent of Socors**, once the centre of the order's council seminary. In summer, the traditional Music Festival and auditions for the renowned **Capella Davídica** choir are held in the cloister. In Plaça de la Llibertat a picturesque open-air market is held daily alongside the newly-built Casa de Cultura. Retracing our steps, in Carrer del Santíssim, are two more interesting palaces: the **Palau of the Dukes of Almenara Alta** and the one of the principal branch of the **Saura** families, part of which has been converted into an antique shop. We can end the route by approaching the hidden Carrer Sant Francesc. This street, along with Carrer de Palau and Carrer de Sant Jeroni, lead to **Carrer Major del Born** form what was once El Call or Jewish quarter.

If until now we have stressed the image of a Ciutadella of convents and palaces, then no less symbolic is that of the **El Born obelisk** when we get into the square via Carrer Major. Built in memory of the victims of the Turkish attack, the shadow it casts, like that of a sundial, points in turn to the many notable buildings that surround the square. To our left as we enter the square, the **Salort** and **Vivó** palaces and, further on, the **convent of Sant Francesc**. To the right, the **Palau of the Count of Torre Saura** with its typical arcade galleries. Just beyond, the **Teatre des Born** and its neighbour, the **Cercle Artístic**. On the next block, to round off the ensemble, the **Town Hall**, built in the 19th century on the site of the Moorish governor's citadel. From the rear of this building there is a magnificent view over the port on the terraced area of the bastion.

On a map we can see that the interior of Sa Contramurada, the area we have been in up to now, opens onto a wide avenue which runs parallel to the bay. This avenue separates Es Born from the city's other open space, the **Plaça dels Pins**, is known as the **Camí de Sant Nicolau** and terminates at the castle of the same name, a 17th century defensive tower. Here, in the forecourt, stands a bust of the Ciutadella-born **Farragut**, navy Admiral during the American Civil War.

The entrance to Ciutadella by sea is not the same since the construction of the new port facilities in Son Blanc, that once achieved, seems yet insufficients. On the other hand, the old port, complete with bridge, almost resembles a Venetian canal and its diminutive proportions have a lot to do with its charm. It is barely a kilometre in length and has an average width of two hundred metres. Towering above, the Born bastion offers a stark background to the waterfront below with its terraces, passers-by, fishing boats and yachts that fill the little port with colourful activity... A *bou* is now entering, a fishing boat, and later the tourist trip boats leave: continuous movement. And this movement must be passed on to the water, which is secretly never still: this produces an unusual meteorological phenomena takes place in the waters of the harbour from time to time, the *rissagues*. The water level drops drastically, to the point of disappearing completely, and then returns like a flash flood with sometimes catastrophic consequences for the moored boats, and even the quayside restaurants, as was the case in 1984 and 2006. It does not happen often though, and scientific studies are being carried out to enable meteorologists to forecast the phenomena and thus minimise damage. From the Born area there are two ways down to the port, Carrer Portal del Mar just behind the Town Hall, or the steps of the Baixada Campllonch which lead towards the **Pla de Sant Joan**, scene of an important part of the famous Sant Joan festivities, and you do not need to get lost to appreciate how lively the city is, despite so much hundreds-of-years-old stone.

ES GIN

Although its origin can be traced to the times of the British domination of the island, this local brew bears little resemblance to English gin, being more similar to the Dutch variety. Only one distillery, Xoriguer, remains today and in their factory in the port one can see the antique stills where the juniper berries continue to be processed in accordance with the traditional recipe that dates from the 18th century. The clay bottles in which gin was originally sold are collectors' pieces nowadays, but Xoriguer does commercialize part of its produce in earthenware replicas, long and with a small handle alongside the neck.

Gin is drunk straight or in combination with herbes, a liqueur made locally from a mixture of wild herbs in which camomile is the most dominant; with a slice of lemon and a splash of soda-water, in which case it is called pallofa; or watered-down with lemon squash as the famous and ostensibly innocuous pomada, the life and soul of Menorcan festivals.

PORT DE MAÓ
SA MESQUIDA
ES GRAU
FAR DE FAVÀRITX
PORT D'ADDAIA

Favàritx lighthouse

Sa Mesquida beach

Talatí de Dalt *taula*

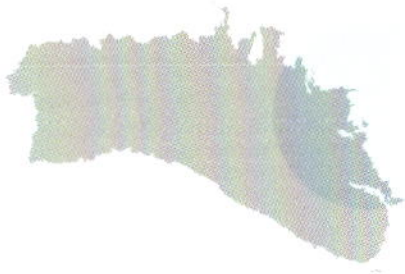

NORTHEAST

FROM **PORT DE MAÓ** TO **NA MACARET**

Port de Maó

The whole north-eastern coast is rugged, with small peninsulas facing the waves with broken cliffs due to the violent action of the sea and the north wind. Es Grau, where the sea joins the saltwater lagoon of the Albufera, and Port d'Addaia which is formed by a natural inlet that extends more than 3km inland, are the only two places of shelter for boats along this stretch of coast. For this reason, sailors are advised to stay on the south side of the island when the wind is from the north, and even the beaches can be hazardous on rough days, despite the attractions of Sa Mesquida, Morella and Tortuga.

S'Albufera d'Es Grau, now a Natural Park, is a humid area of great biological interest, inhabited by many species of water fowl. In summer they make their nests and raise their young and it is an important port of call on the migratory routes. The lagoon is separated from the open sea by banks of reeds, pines and sabine trees.

Cap de Favàritx, with its lighthouse overlooking a landscape of harsh black slate, is a tremendous contrast to the gently rolling hills of S'Albufera, particularly on stormy days when it takes on an almost Dantesque appearance. Despite this a visit is highly recommended.

Between this coastline and the town of Alaior, the countryside is comprised of woodlands of evergreen oak and pine trees which alternate with rock formations of varied and curious forms, such as the Penyes d'Egipte or the Capell de Ferro, and is an ideal area for walking on a hot day.

Es Grau

EXCURSIONS
BY FOOT
OR BY BICYCLE

NORTHEAST

FROM
PORT DE MAÓ
TO
NA MACARET

1
Sa Mesquida
Es Grau

2
Es Grau
Sa Torreta

3
Camí de de Sa Boval
Sa Torreta
de Tramuntana

4
Es Puntarró
Binixems

5
Camí de
Mongofre Nou

6
Favàritx
Cala Morella

Conventional signs
Lighthouse
Defence tower
Beaches
Panoramic view
Commercial harbour
Recreational harbour
Fishing harbour
Quarries of marès
Mill
Old chapel, church
Camping
Filling station
Airport
Aerodrome
Talaiotic settlement
Taula
Talaiot
Naveta
Caves
Early-christian basilica
Main road
Secondary road
Paved track
Urbanization road
Unmade track
Narrow path
Brook
Camí de Cavalls
Excursions
Natural Park
of S'Albufera des Grau
Cap de Favàritx
Cala Presili
Platja de Capifort
Platja d'en Tortuga
Cap d' en Tortuga
Cala Morella Nou
Cap de Mossén Vives
Cala en Cavaller
Morro de sa Falconera
es Caló de s'Oli
Punta de ses Àligues
Cap de Mestral
Cala de sa Torreta
Torre de Rambla
Cala des Tamarells
Illa d'en Colom
Cap de LLevant
Punta Fra Bernat
Platja des Grau
Illots de sa Cudia
Punta de sa Cudia
Punta de sa Galera
Es Grau
Parc Natural s'Albufera des Grau
s'Albufera
sa Cudia Nova
es Violar
ses Salvatges Primes
Caló de ses Mandries
Cala Grau
ses Salvatges Fondes
Caleta de Binillautí
ses Piquetes
Macar de Binillautí
en Bombarda
s' Esquena d'Ase
sa Raconada Vella
es Pa Gros
Illots de sa Mesquida
Cala Mesquida
Torre de sa Mesquida
Punta de sa Bateria Vella
Sa Mesquida
Punta Negre
Cala es Murtar
Es Murtar
Cap Negre
els Escullots
ses Àligues
Punta de ses Bancades
es Freus
la Mare de Déu
Punta de s'Esperó
la Mola
Punta de na Nega James
es Clot
Castell de Sant Felip
Punta de Sant Carles
Cala Sant Esteve
Fort Malborough
Sant Antoni
Cala Llonga
Illa del Rei
Maó
Son Vilar
Es Castell
Horizonte
Santa Ana
Sol del Este
Noria Riera
Illa del Llatzeret
Llucmaçanes
Aeroclub de Sant Lluís
Serra Morena
Binisarmenya
Sant Isidre
sa Granja
Pla dels Vergers
Sant Joan dels Vergers
Son Petit
Alfavaret
Cala de s'Enclusa
Punta de s'Enclusa
Cala Pou d'en Caldés
Macar d'Enmig
Punta de sa Font
Macar de sa Roba
Punta Timons
es Portitxol
s'Escala
Favàritx
Capifort
Morella
sa Torreta
Torre Blanca
sa Torre Blanca
es Prat
Binillautí
Binillautí Nou
Binillautí Vell
Santa Rita
Sant Bartomeu
Morella Nou
Morella Vell
Santa Mariana
Ermita de Fátima
sa Boaleta
sa Boal Vella
es Palmer Vell
Sant Ramon
s'Esqueller
es Planàs
Son Mir
Palafanguer de Baix
Palafanguer de sa Barrera
na Bona
Milà Nou
Milà Vell
Estància de Milà
Rafal Nou
Rafal Vell
Algarrova
Algarrovet
Lliberto Vell
Agotars
Rafal Colom
Biniarroga
Biniarroga Nou
Biniaixa
Ka n e
Cornia
Curniola
es Fornàs
Torelló
na Ferranda
sa Cúdia Cremada
Santa Margarida
Trepucó
Robadones
Son Tuduri
sa Casa Nova
Santa Anna
Son Granot
Son Biali
Son Amat
s' Ereta
Bintaufa Vell
na Xenxa d'en Borràs
Biniarroca
Hipòdrom
Sant Llorenç
Torre Vella
Toraixa des Pi
Cap de Favàritx
GR 223
Me-1
Me-3
Me-5
Me-7
Me-8
Me-12
Me-14
Me-2
Me-6
Cf-1
Cf-2
81
92
72
0
1
1 km
N

Cala en Vidrier, facing Es Grau

Cala des Tamarells

Torreta de Tramuntana *taula*

1

Sa Mesquida Es Grau

As this walk follows a clearly defined path except for occasional, short stretches, it presents no difficulty but does require some stamina and, in summer, a hat or sunshade and drinking water, but it is highly recommendable because it enables you to discover a section of virtually unspoilt coastline despite being very close to Maó. The path runs along the high part of the cliffs, offering wonderful views of the open sea, only interrupted by charming little coves that are perfect for a swim. The track is wide and easy to follow and is a pathway in just a few sections. We advise you, however, to organise your return trip by car, bus or taxi from **Es Grau**.

—

Time approx.: 3-4h (one-way)

2

Es Grau Sa Torreta

The starting point is the small wooden bridge that leads onto the beach of **Es Grau**. Cross to the other side of the bridge and take the path that starts there. After a small cove with a cottage we have to leave the path that goes towards the left and continue behind the **Punta de Fra Bernat**. The slowly climbing route provides excellent views of the **Illa d'en Colom**. Until we reach **Cala de Sa Torreta** the landscape is one of rolling hills to the east of **S'Albufera**. The return trip is made by retracing our steps.

—

Time approx.: 2h (return)

3

Sa Boval – Sa Torreta de Tramuntana

The **Camí de Sa Boval** crosses an extension of farmland which once formed part of the **S'Albufera** marshlands. The archaeological site at **Torreta de Tramuntana**, complete with *naveta*, remains of a settlement and *taula* (the only one with a sea view), offers lovely panoramic views of the coast and the **Illa d'en Colom**. Is one of the excursions that enable us to discover the island's interior. Visits are only allowed on Thursdays from 9 a.m. to 1 p.m. You should leave the vehicle at the entrance to the path that leads to the estate.

—

Time approx.: 2h 30m (return)

Sant Llorenç de Binixems hermitage

Es Capell de Ferro

Presili beach

4

Es Puntarró Binixems

Starting from the same flat area described in the previous excursion, we follow the path towards higher ground and a protected zone of rich woodland (included in the protected areas), arriving eventually at the hermitage of **Sant Llorenç de Binixems**, one of the island's oldest, built at the time of the Catalan conquest in the 13th century and mentioned in the Treaty of Anagni as one of the parishes that had to form part of the new territorial organisation.

—

Time approx.: 2h 30m (return)

5

Camí de Mongofre Nou

A simple "there and back" walk takes us from the main road to the entrance of the **Mongofre Nou** estate, which is closed to the public, and back. On the way we can see the curious rock formations of **Capell de Ferro** (Iron Hat) to the west of the path. Also possible by car. You can continue on foot along the Camí de Cavalls as far as the old saltworks of Port d'Addaia.

—

Time approx.: Less than 1h

6

Favàritx Cala Morella

After exploring the interesting scenery of the **Cap de Favàritx** headland surrounding the lighthouse, we return to **Presili** and **Tortuga**. An area of dunes and marshlands (usually dry in summer) lies just behind the beach. Our objective is to reach **Morella Nou**, crossing the headland that separates the two beaches. On this walk we will come across a great variety of terrains and natural environments.

—

Time approx.: 1h 30m (return)

Port de Maó

Es Castell | Cales Fonts

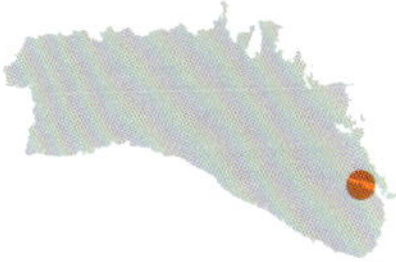

Above, the **Port of Maó**, whose natural harbour stretches inland for 5km, provides magnificent natural shelter. A walk along cornice from the city provides an extensive view, and a boat trip around the port offers another highly recommendable perspective.

Clustered around the bay, **Es Castell** enjoys the honour of being the first town in Spain to see the sun rise every morning. In contrast, the old fishing port of **Cales Fonts** has become a busy nucleus of bars and restaurants that fill to capacity on summer nights.

Sa Mesquida

Es Pa Gros | Sa Raconada Vella

The Es Pa Gros headland, 68m high, overlooks **Cala Mesquida**. The French landed here to occupy the island in 1871. At the opposite extreme of the beach, we see the Sa Mesquida defence tower, built by the British at the end of the 18th century as protection against further surprise attacks.

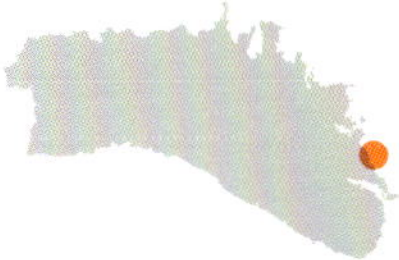

To the north of **Es Pa Gros** a second quieter cove appears, known as **Sa Raconada Vella**. Fewer people come here as there is far less sand.

To the left of this panoramic view appears the initial nucleus of cottages where, among others, many locals from Maó have traditionally spent their summer holidays.

Es Grau
Natural Park of S'Albufera

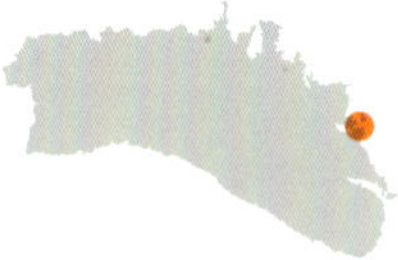

The magnificent landscape of **Es Grau** with its ample beach and traditional houses to one side and the **Illa d'en Colom** to the other, has benefited from the declaration of **S'Albufera** as the island's first nature reserve. The unique character of this sizeable ecological zone is now recognised and guarantees the end of further property developments in a very valuable habitat, due to the bird life and many species of plants, as well as enabling scientific and educational projects to be undertaken.

Es Grau
S'Albufera | Es Tamarells | Illa d'en Colom

A walk around the signposted routes of the **S'Albufera Natural Park** emphasises the importance of this marshland zone that forms part of the migratory routes of many European and African birds. It is connected to the sea by the narrow Sa Gola canal.

Another place of interest in this area is the quiet and secluded **Cala des Tamarells** which can only be reached on foot from Es Grau. (Itinerary 2 on page 46).

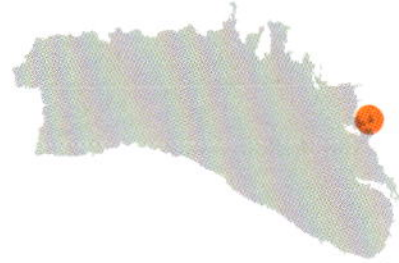

If you have your own boat, you can go from Es Grau to the **Illa d'en Colom** as another very interesting option.

The **Caló des Moro** is one of the two small but attractive beaches to be found on the islet.

Far de Favàritx
Morella Nou | Cala en Tortuga

Close to Favàritx, the lovely unspoilt cove of **Morella Nou** is surrounded by pinewoods and a typical old boathouse stands on the beach. It can be reached following the itinerary 6 on page 47.

Behind **Capifort**, in the photo, there are not very extensive dune formations and marshlands, **Es Prat**.

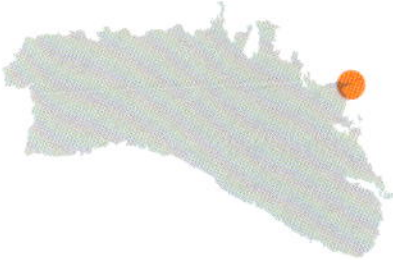

The silhouette of the **Favàritx** lighthouse overlooks the black slate, almost lunar, landscape of the most desolate headland of the eastern coast. On stormy days, the sea breaking over the rocks is a breathtaking sight.

Port d'Addaia
Mongofre | Na Macaret

The rugged outline of this part of the coast gives rise to hidden treasures such as the coves of **S'Enclusa** and **Mongofre**.

In the inner part of the Port of Addaia, can still be seen the structure of ancient salt-works.

At the entrance to the long and narrow **Port d'Addaia** you can see the installations of the sports port protected by the islet of **Ses Mones**. In the background, the cottages of **Na Macaret** and the islets of **Addaia**.

ARENAL D'EN CASTELL
ARENAL DE SON SAURA
FORNELLS
CAP DE CAVALLERIA
CALA PREGONDA

Near Es Mercadal

Arenal de Son Saura (Son Parc)

Cala Pregonda

NORTH

FROM **ARENAL D'EN CASTELL** TO **CALA PREGONDA**

Port de sa Nitja

Es Mercadal is the geographic heart of this area, and Fornells its tourist centre. Its enormous bay, protected from the north wind and the sea by the Sa Mola promontory, is the ideal setting for all kinds of water sports. The nearby beaches, such as Binimel·là, are restful contrasts to the rest of the rugged coastline and Pregonda, because of its inaccessibility, remains hidden to all but the most determined visitors.

Owing to its very varied geological characteristics, it is impossible to generalize about the nature of this landscape: in Cala Roja, in the bay of Fornells, there are copper-coloured formations (typical of the Triassic era also seen at the famous Penya del Indi or at Cavalleria, where there is also a Cap Roig) that are completely unrelated to the grey or black formations found close by. There is, however, one definitive common factor – the tramuntana wind – that, in combination with the violent action of the waves it creates, erodes and changes the shape of all it touches.

This whole coastline has been declared a protected area under the Balearic Islands Natural Spaces legislation. There are other interesting points inland as well; Sta. Àgueda, with its Moorish fortification, and El Toro are the two great vantage points of the island, and the countryside that lies between them, almost untouched by man, seems to have suffered no greater transformations than those imposed by the changing seasons.

Fornells

EXCURSIONS
BY FOOT
OR BY BICYCLE

NORTH

FROM
ARENAL
D'EN CASTELL
TO
CALA PREGONDA

7
Arenal de Son Saura
Cala Pudent

8
Cala Roja

9
Ferragut beach
Binimel·là beach

10
Binimel·là beach
Cala Pregonda

11
Ferreries
Camí de Ruma

12
Santa Àgueda

des Porros
es Cobrómbol
Cap de Cavalleria
Cova d'en Mora
Far de Cavalleria
es Pas
89
s'Olla
Cap Roig
uera d'en John
Cala Viola de Ponent
Port de Sanitja
na Blanca
Punta d'en Batista
Punta de sa Torre
Cala Viola de Llevant
Punta des Vernís
sa Talaia
es Marès
sa Trona
Cala Torta
Sanitja
Punta de sa Cova de ses Ovelles
Cavalleria
9
Santa Teresa
es Macar Gran
Punta Negra
Coll de sa Cabra
Punta Mala
Cap de Fornells
na Ponça
sa Selleta
es Morter
Cova dels Anglesos
es Jugador de Plè
Punta de na Guillemassa
122
Mola de Fornells
Cova des Orgues
Cova de na Polida
Cap d'en Pentinar
Torre de Fornells
Castell de Sant Antoni
Clot des Guix
es Xiprer
Punta de sa Talaieta
Cala Tirant
Fornells
Platges de Fornells
Cala Tirant
Illa d'en Tosqueta
Macar d'en Tosqueta
Cap Negre
na Fonoll
Niu de Xòrics
Illa Sargantana
Illa des Revells
Cala Pudent
Arenal de Son Saura
ses Olles
Cap des Redoble
Punta Grossa
Cavalleria
127
Binidonaire
Binidonairet
Arenal de Tirant
Tirant Nou
Badia de Fornells
Cala Rotja
ses Salines
es Carregador
s Martinells
Estància d'en Magister
ses Cases Noves
Almudaina
51
ses Casetes Noves
Tirant Vell
Cala Blanca
7
GR 223
Macar de sa Llosa
Arenal d'en Castell
Punta Grossa
Pesquera d'Enmig
Punta de na Ferradura
Racó de na Ferradura
Punta d'en Siulet
Illa Petita d'Addaia
riac Nou
Lluriac Vell
es Prat
Vilanova
sa Concepció
ses Salines Noves
Santa Victòria
8
Me-7
s'Albufera
83
Cap des Port
s'Albufera
Son Parc
Arenal d'en Castell
Marina de Bellavista
Na Macaret
Coves Noves
Cala Molí
Me-9
Cala Molí
Torrent des Mercadal
Binisarret
Binisarraia
Binicreixent
Bellamirada de Dalt
Bellamirada Vella
Mota Gran
Pujol Roig
94
s'Hort de Llucatx
Cala Molí
101
Addaia
Torre d'Addaia
Estància de Montpalau
Estància de Barbatx
Barbatx
Montpalau
Barbatx
Me-15
Estància d'en Siano
Son Servera
Sant Joan de Carbonell
Sant Joan des Horts
Estància de Sant Diego
Llucatx
Coves Velles
ses Coves Noves
Me-11
ses Coves Velles
Port d'Addaia
en Brut
es Caragol
Me-7
Penya des Corb
ses Fontanilles
Savinar de Mongofre
Binigurdó
190
Llucatx
Molinet
Hort des Lleó
Mongofre Nou
Addaia
Llinàritx Nou
Peu del Toro
l'Enzell
235
sa Roca
Binifabini
Son Làdico
ses Salines
GR 223
es Mercadal
x Vell
Rafalet Nou
Me-13
el Toro
358
Mare de Déu del Toro
Puig de s'Ermità
238
Albaida
172
Binifabini
Son Tema
es Xalet
sa Farinera
Rafal des Frares
Roca des Frare
202
Puig Mal
214
Puig Mal
Santa Eulàlia de Dalt
Son Alzina
Santa Maria
Capell de Ferro
92
Alcotx
Planes de s'Albaida
Estància d'Alcotx
Binimatzoc
Me-7
Santa Rosa
Binifailla
s'Arangí
s'Aranjassa
Binillubet
Estància d'en Rovella
Estància de Binillubet
Me-9
s'Albaida
Estància de Sant Pere
Binixems
Santa Catalina de Dalt
Binissegui
es Pi
Santa Eularieta
Binixems de Darrera
Son Gall
Egipte
nt Redona
Dalt
Sant Jeroni
Estància d'en Nofre
Son Puig
Santa Bàrbara
Sant Llorenç de Binixems
Binixems de Devant
Estància Cucanya
Son Benet
na Vermella
es Banyu
Sant Joan
s'Artiga Vella
ses Penyes
Hort de Son Trémol
Me-16
Estància de Sant Josep
Estància des Borinot
s'Artigueta
Camp Siquiat
Son Planes
Puig Menor
Estància de ses Penyes
Turmaden
Sant Josep
Estància Camí del Toro
Son Roca
es Camp Siquiat
Torrent des Puntarró
112
es Bec Nou
es Bec Vell
Estància de Binixebonet
Me-1
Biniguarda Vell
Biniguarda Nou
Riu de la Plata
Estància de Biniac
sa Cova de Baix
es Becs
Santa Creu
Biniatzau
es Tres Jurats
Son Torres
s'Almudaina
Biniguarda
Llimpet
Son Bonaventura
Puig Menor Nou
Son Blanc Vell
Binixebó
Binixebonet
Santa Magdalena
es Cos
la Cova
Llimpa
Alaior
Borrassos Nou
Sant Miquel
es Barranquet
Vil·la Tanús
La Trotxa
es Biniacs
Morell
Catalina
Vell
Son Blanc Nou
Santa Ponça
Santa Ponça
sa Mola
Llumena Nou
es Llumenes
Biniac Nou
es Canumet
es Canum
es Canum
N
0
1
1 km

Cala Pudent

Cala Roja

Cattle in Tramontana

7

Arenal de Son Saura Cala Pudent

From the small cove of Els Alocs and along a path that borders the coast half way up the cliff, we reach one of the most loved beaches by those who hate the madding crowds, and one of the few with a freshwater spring. Going towards the east (you have to leave Punta des Carregador between us and the sea), we come across a curious work of nature: hundreds of rocks have been eroded by the sea to form pebbles of such disproportionate size that the beach they form has the appearance of a giant's playground, Pla de Mar..

—

Time approx.: Less than 1h (return)

8

Cala Roja

It starts shortly before the crossroads of the Me-7 and the Me-15 (Es Mercadal-Fornells). For 2.2 km we follow the Camí de Cavalls which we leave taking a turn to the left, to go through a pine wood until the unusual geological formations of **Cala Roja**. The characteristic, red clay flats which give the beach its name (rotja meaning red in Catalan) are a popular site for skin-cleansing mud baths or simply for enjoying the splendid view of the great bay of Fornells. The best way to return is by following the coastline via **Cala Blanca** and, on arrival at the saltworks and old house at La Concepción, take the path that leads back to our point of departure. Keen walkers can lengthen the route discovering the small paths that go round La Mola de Fornells from here.

—

Time approx.: 1h 30m (return)

9

Cavalleria beach Binimel·là beach

Starting from either of these beaches, this pleasant, easy walk enables us to discover this stretch of the coastline and **Cala Mica**, a cove that lies between the two.

—

Time approx.: 1h 30m (return)

Cala Pregonda

Rural landscape

The path to Santa Àgueda

10

Binimel·là beach Cala Pregonda

A short walk along the coastline from **Binimel·là** beach, this is the best way to discover the beautiful **Cala Pregonda**.

—

Time approx.:
Less than 1h (return)

11

Ferreries Camí de Ruma

Heading north from Ferreries, the **Camí de Ruma** crosses the Hort de Sant Patrici estate and, after a succession of uphill bends, we arrive at Sant Francesc where we must leave the car and take the unmade path to the right which will afford us excellent and unusual views of both the north and south coasts on either side. Beyond Sant Josep, the pathway becomes a rough track but presents no difficulty, and the rest of the circuit, which coincides partly with the **Camí de Tramuntana**, is easy to follow, becoming steeper beyond Sant Antoni de Ruma. During this last stretch we can enjoy good views of **Sta. Àgueda** and **S'Enclusa**.

—

Time approx.: 3h 30m (return)

12

Santa Àgueda

An ancient cobblestone road leads us to the top of the mountain at 264m above sea level where the most notable traces of the Moorish domination of the island are to be found in the form of a ruined fort. It has been declared part of the National Historic and Artistic Heritage and a restoration plan of the old fortress and chapel is being undertaken. Spectacular views.

—

Time approx.: 1h 30m (return)

Due to its characteristics, more similar to the south, **Cala Pregonda** is a unique spot on the north coast.

Arenal d'en Castell
Macar de Sa Llosa

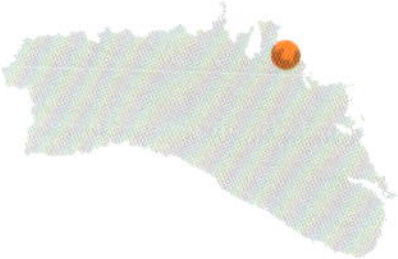

Arenal d'en Castell, with its many hotels and tourist developments, is protected from the east wind by the stone mass of Punta Grossa. This is one of the island's most popular beaches.

The **Macar de sa Llosa** is another lovely spot lying within the same great bay as Arenal d'en Castell, from where it may be reached on foot. Access is easier, however, from Son Parc, an urbanisation situated further north.

Arenal de Son Saura
Cala Pudent | Fornells

Arenal de son Saura is frequently called Son Parc, partly in reference to the tourist complex that now surrounds it, and partly in order to distinguish it from the south coast Son Saura cove. Behind the sandy area is a large stretch of dunes, and further inland is the island's only golf course.

The tiny **Cala Pudent** lies to the left of Son Saura. Its proximity to the sands of the Arenal and the beauty of the surroundings make it an attractive place to visit (See itinerary 7, page 64).

The Mola de **Fornells** is a natural barrier between the north and north-eastern coasts. As such, the rocky headland stands as an impressive retaining wall against the violence of the sea and the fierce tramuntana, with this type of large saltwater lake that forms the extensive and closed bay.

The whole area, currently protected as a natural reserve has often been at the point of being subjected to big transformations, but fortunately its charms have not been undermined by the spread of urbanisation.

Fornells
Ses Salines | Cala Tirant

The fishing village of **Fornells**, in constant growth, has become an important tourist centre. The lobster stews served here in the restaurants have a lot to do with its popularity. In the background, it can be seen the watchtower built by the British after the demolition of the Sant Antoni fort.

The installations of the old saltworks of **Ses Salines** can be seen at the end of the enormous bay of Fornells. Alongside, it seems as if the pinewood wants to refresh itself in the waters of **Cala Blanca**. This scenery forms part of the area visited on itinerary 8 (see page 64).

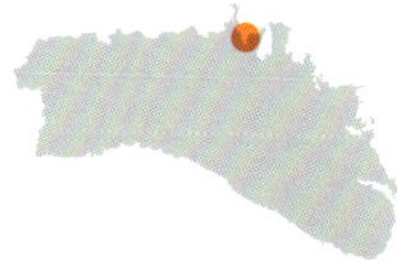

The coastline opposite the quayside is dotted with tiny coves which emphasise the impression of a land-locked sea affording ideal conditions for sailing sports of all kinds.

In **Cala Tirant**, the name of a new urbanisation, Playas de Fornells, confirms the fact that the townspeople consider this to be "their" beach. Beyond the sand, there is a marshland zone and tamarisk trees.

Cap de Cavalleria
Ferragut | Sanitja | Binimel·là

The **Cavalleria** peninsula ends at this headland, where the lighthouse marks the northernmost point of the island. The **Illa dels Porros**, seen here on the horizon, is often covered by the raging sea.

The beaches of **Cavalleria** and **Ferragut** with their red sands are ideal for bathing as long as the wind is not from the north. From here to the nearby beach of Binimel·la it is a pleasant, short walk as described in the itinerary 9 on page 64.

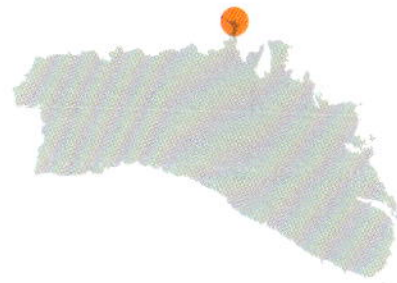

Another view of the **Cavalleria** headland allows us to appreciate the different configuration of the two versants: high cliffs to the east and more gentle slopes down to the sea to the west. On the right we see the small harbour of **Sanitja**.

Binimel·là beach is the largest and most easily accessible in an area that is well-known for the richness of its marine floor. The adjacent land, such as Es Pla Vermell, owes much of its fertility to the presence of fresh water springs.

Cala Pregonda
Pregondó

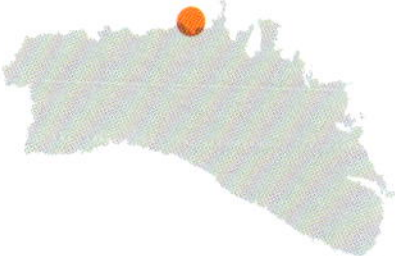

Cala Pregonda

Illes Bledes | Cala Barril | Cala Calderer

Inaccessibility by road has enabled **Pregonda** to remain unspoilt, conserving its idyllic combination of fine sands, transparent waters and surrounding pinewoods. The beauty of the setting is enhanced even more by its location in the centre of the rugged and inhospitable north coast. (See excursion 10 page 65).

The rocks that lie just offshore protect the cove from the open sea creates an atmosphere reminiscent of other lands. The wider area of sand on the left of the photo is known as **Pregondó**.

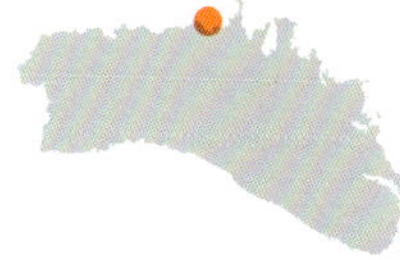

Cala Barril is protected by another rocky crag. The larger of the **Bledes** islets undoubtedly marks the extreme of the underwater prolongation of the headland.

Another lovely spot on this part of the coastline, **Cala Calderer**, forms part of one of the island's largest protected areas of special interest. Reaching here is only possible via the Camí de Cavalls, or with some type of boat, but it is a good excuse to discover the setting.

CALA PILAR
ALGAIARENS
CIUTADELLA
CAP D'ARTRUTX
SON SAURA
MACARELLA

The beaches of Algaiarens

Ciutadella. Torre-Saura

Cala Macarelleta

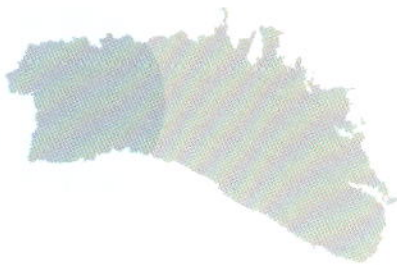

WEST

FROM **CALA PILAR** TO **CALA MACARELLA**

The western extreme of Menorca, which coincides with the municipal district of Ciutadella, is the driest and most barren part of the island and is bordered, to the north, by the green belt of La Vall and, to the south, by the gorges or ravines. It takes the shape of a great platform which slopes progressively down towards the south coast.

The main points of scenic interest are along the coast while inland there are many prehistoric monuments and in terms of rural architecture some fine examples of wealthy landowners' mansions that remain today as evidence of past affluence.

The accesses to the beaches which on the south coast have escaped the urbanising process, go through private estates on their final section. The limitations for passing imposed by their owners meant that for a period of time they were infrequently visited. The current free access means that there are queues in the summer season to reach the famous "unspoilt coves": Son Saura, Es Talaier, En Turqueta and Macarella

Nevertheless, thease beaches should be used, or towards Algaiarens on the north coast, if you want to escape from the development closest to Ciutadella: Santandria, Cala en Blanes, Cala en Brut, Cala en Forcat, Cales Piques... which are also of interest and well serviced.

The undeniable personality of Ciutadella as a historic city surpasses it value as the main junction to the whole area. Its markedly Mediterranean character, the charm of its streets and stately buildings are aspects to be taken into account when organising a special visit.

Cala en Blanes

EXCURSIONS
BY FOOT
OR BY BICYCLE

WEST

FROM
CALA PILAR
TO
CALA MACARELLA

13

Els Alocs
Cala Pilar

14

Cala Galdana
Cala Macarella
Cala en Turqueta

15

Torre Trencada
Algendar gorge

16

Punta de s'Escullar

17

Son Xoriguer
Es Talaier

Cala Morell
Punta Llevant de Cala Morell
Cova de sa Merda
Pont des Colomar
Punta de Fra Bernat
Penyal de Curniola
Cova d'en Guàrdia
Codolar de Biniatram
Punta Rotja
Cala en Carbó
Penyal des Frare
Cap Gros
Racó de s'Alga
Racó de s'Aram
Caló d'en Sintes
Racó de ses Xàvegues
Penyals de sa Falconera
Caló d'Alfurinet
Punta de l'Anticrist
Penyals de sa Muntanya Mala
Macar d'Alfurinet
Punta des Carregador
Cala del Pilar
Cala dels Alocs
Roca de sa Sal
Cala Moragues
Cala en Calderer
Punta cala en Calderer
Curniola
CALA MORELL
Cala d'Algaiarens
Algaiarens
132
sa Muntanya Mala
198
sa Falconera
207
Pla de Mar
GR 223
13
Penyals de Binidalfà
140
114
Son Ermità
Son Morell
Morell Nou
Curniola
Pinar de Son Angel
Coves de l'Amo en Marc
Santa Elisabet
Algaiarens
sa Vinya
Penya de sa Miloca
la Vall
s'Hort de la Vall
s'Hort de sa Font Santa
Pla de sa Font
Biniatram
sa Font Santa
Alfurinet
Sant Felip
Bintidalfà
Son Serra
Son Seu
Son Morell de Baix
Canal de l'Infern
Alfurí de Dalt
Torre d'en Quart
Son Angel
Alfurí de Baix
Santa Àgueda
260
Castell de Santa Àgueda
Son Abatzer
Binigafull
s'Almudaina
16
Son Planas
Son Bernat
ses Arenes
Binicanó
Alqueria Blanca
Alquerieta
Son Bruc
Santa Cecília
es Caragolí
ses Arenes
Binisuesets
ses Arenetes
Santa Victòria
Alpútzer Vell
Alpútzer Nou
Binimoti
Son Quart
Son Pebre
els Aljubs
Binisues
es Tripol
Coll Roig
222
Santa Bàrbara
Son Bauló
Puig de ses Paisses
Me-1
ses Angoixes
Rafal Nou
Naveta des Tudons
ses Tavernes
Son Toni Martí
190
Santa Bàrbara
Santa Magdalena
Puig de Santa Magdalena
Santa Teresa
228
Puig de sa Torre
Na Marcona
Sant Tomàs
es Tudons
Son Sintes
ses Païsses
249
Torrellafuda
sa Muntanyeta
137
s'Enclusa
Son Pons
Muntanya Vella
Son Bell-Lloc
276
Binigarba
Son Camps
Son Aparets
Son Bell-Lloc Vell
Cavalleria Vella
Cavalleria Nova
Torrellafuda
Son Bell-Lloquet nou
Son Blanc
Binipati Nou
Torretrencada
Sant Joan
ses Delícies
Sans
sa Trinitat
Cavallerieta
Sobrevell
FERRERIES
15
Torrerencada
Binipati Veil
Tot Lluc
Son Gornés
179
Son Olives
es Canaló
Son Guillem
Biniatrum
sa Beltrana
142
es Canavallons
Torre Saura
es Pas d'en Revull
Bellaventura
Tot Lluquet
Gornesset
Morvedre Vell
Escola
Son Febrer
es Torretó
Sant Antoni de S'Aranjassa
Sant Joan de Missa
Pabordia Nova
Me-22
Estància de Son Mercer
Morvedre Nou
Algendar Nou
Algendar Vell
Son Martorell
Calafí Nou
Puig de Son Tica
Torre Petxina Vella
Pabordia Vella
Torre Petxina Nova
Binimassó
Rosa
91
Torre Petxina
Binicalsitx
Sant Joan Gran
Son Foc
116
Son Mercer de Baix
Son Tica
Torralbet
Algendaret
Son Triay
Santa Elena
Calafí Vell
Santa Galdana
Son Piris
Son Fonoll
Son Camaró
Lloc Nou
el Pare
Son Mestres de Dalt
es Barrancó
Catlar
Torralba
Santa Maria
Binicalsitx
Son Catlar
es Clot
Son Alzina
Son Mestres Nou
Barranc de sa Cova
Santa Ponça
Sant Josep
Son Mercer de Baix
Son Vecete
sa Marjaleta
el Pericó
es Calafat
Son Olivar
Son Carabassa
Son Tarí Nou
Santa Aina
SERPENTONA
ses Cases de s'Hort
Sant Llorenç
s'Hort de Binissaid
sa Marjal Nova
s'Alzinar
sa Cova
sa Marjal Vella
Macarella
14
Sant Francesc
es Bèrecs
Mitjaneta
CALA GALDANA
Torre Saura Vell
na Llarga
GR 223
Horts de Trebalúger
Mallauí
Bellavista
ses Pedreres
Talaia d'Artrutx
64
sa Teulera
els Banyuls
es Boueret
Saura Nou
Barranc de Macarella
Barranc d'Algendar
Barranc de Trebalúger
Platges de Son Saura
Punta des Governador
Cala des Talaier
Punta de na Bruna
Cala en Turqueta
na Foradada
Penyes d'Alpericó
Punta de na Gall
es Castellet
Cala Macarelleta
Cala Macarella
Cova des Boc
ses Alegries
Cala Galdana
S'Enfonsat de Binissaid
Cala Mitjana
es Pont de n'Alí
Cova Foradada
Cala Trebalúger
Pas de s'Arrel
Esquena de s'Ase
Cala Fustam
Cala Escorxada
es Canal Gran
Punta de na Rabiosa
es Calons

Cala Pilar

Cala Mitjana

13

Els Alocs
Cala Pilar

From the small cove of **Els Alocs** and along a path that borders the coast half way up the cliff, we reach one of the most loved beaches by those who hate the madding crowds, and one of the few with a freshwater spring. Going towards the east (you have to leave Punta des Carregador between us and the sea), we come across a curious work of nature: hundreds of rocks have been eroded by the sea to form pebbles of such disproportionate size that the beach they form has the appearance of a giant's playground, **Pla de Mar**.

—

Time approx.: 2h (return)

14

Cala Galdana
Cala Macarella
Cala en Turqueta

The first stretch of the path is separated from the sea by pine woods. The beautiful coves of **Macarella** and **Macarelleta** are, in themselves, well worth the trip, but, after a refreshing swim there, it is advisable to carry on as far as **Cala en Turqueta**. If we wish to complete our discovery of the area, we can combine this walk with number 17, doing it the other way round and adding another half hour (for the section between the two) to the total time.

—

Time approx.: 2h 30m (return)

Torretrencada taula

Rock formations near Cala Morell

Es Talaier

15

Torretrencada Algendar gorge

Leaving Ciutadella on the Camí Vell de Maó, we will make a first stop at **Torretrencada** to visit the *talaiot* and *taula*. The site is well signposted and there is a car park. It is possible to reach the neighbouring village of Torrellafuda on foot, where there is another area of Taulas. We then continue along the path in the same direction until then, turn left when there is a fork and go on until it is no longer asphalted, at the point of Son Guillem. We will leave the car where the tarmac road ends and continue, on foot, to the **Barranc** (gorge) **d'Algendar**. The old pathway, excavated out of the rock and still paved with cobblestones in places, leads us on an attractive walk to the gorge of the river bed, passing through luxuriant vegetation.

—

Time approx.: 1h (return) for the part on foot

16

Punta de S'Escullar

This short excursion brings us into contact with the north-east coast, which is rugged and solitary, except for specific points such as the nearby **Cala Morell**. Vehicles must be left where the asphalt finishes, and good views of the cliffs are to be had from the headland just beyond the road's end.

—

Time approx.: 1h (return)

17

Son Xoriguer Es Talaier

You can also start in Cala en Bosc, crossing the urbanised sector that separates it from **Son Xoriguer**. It is always close to the sea and you only have to go over a few barriers. Passing the estate of So na Parets Nou, to the left of the path, and beyond the entrance to Torre Saura Vell, we come to the double sandy area of **Son Saura**. Following the Camí de Cavalls, on passing the Punta des Governador, we reach **Es Talaier**, a cove of fine, white sand but very much smaller than Son Saura. It is possible to extend this route with number 14, shown before.

—

Time approx.: 3h 30m (return)

Cala Pilar
Cala Carbó

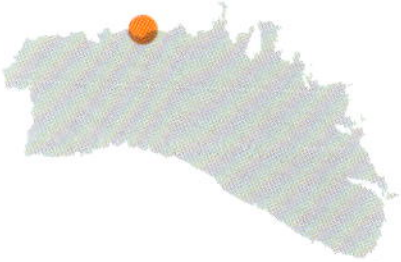

Although there is a good half an hour's walk to **Cala Pilar** (or perhaps for this very reason, as it discourages the majority of possible visitors) this beach, on the right and previous page, is one of the most popular among those who wish to escape from the crowds. To the left of the beach, an interesting cove of giant pebbles, eroded by the sea over the centuries. (See excursion 13 page 82).

Cala Carbó is another hideaway for connoisseurs of the north coast. The best route of access is by boat or from the neighbouring Cala Algaiarens.

Algaiarens
Cala Morell | Punta Nati

The ensemble formed by the beaches of **Es Bot** and **Es Tancat – Algaiarens –** and that of **Ses Fontanelles**, is the high spot of one of the most interesting areas of Menorca, coinciding with the **La Vall** estate.

In **Algaiarens**, the beauty of the surrounding landscape of sand dunes and marshland combines with the clean sands and transparent waters to create an idyllic spot for bathing.

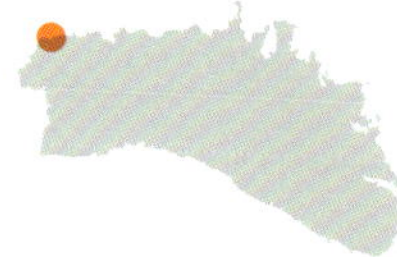

The deep inlet of **Cala Morell** offers a welcome refuge to sailors on a stretch of increasingly rugged coastline. Among the houses of the new development, a few prehistoric caves remain as proof that the cove has been inhabited by man since time immemorial.

Punta Nati is a desolate region; the lighthouse stands on a cliff that drops abruptly to the sea and nothing but the sparsest of vegetation grows among the rocks. The only buildings are *ponts*, curious stone constructions that were used as shelters for livestock... though the selfsame desolation of the spot makes it a really impressive place to see.

Cala en Forcat

Pont d'en Gil | Cala en Blanes

Beyond **Cap de Bajolí**, the westernmost point of the island, the natural archway of **Pont d'en Gil** appears like the secret doorway to a hidden cove.

To the north of Ciutadella, tourist developments rise like fortifications that want to defend their exclusivity around the narrow inlet of **Cala en Forcat**.

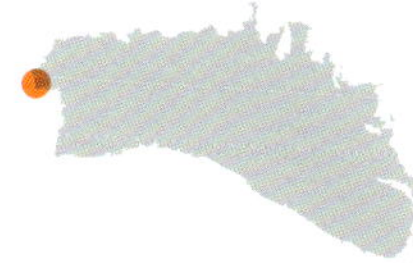

Cala en Brut is almost an estuary with hardly any sand, but sunbathers make use of the concrete platforms that litter the banks so they can toast themselves beneath the summer sun.

Cala en Blanes is wider and deeper than the previous coves, but, even so, in summer they all hang up the "full" sign due to their closeness to Ciutadella.

Ciutadella

The Gothic cathedral has always been the centre point of the old **Ciutadella**, and is the unmovable testimony of the important role it has had representing this city in the history of Menorca. Around it, however, growth is unstoppable and, among other aspects, has led to the creation of a network of roads around the city and new port facilities in the area of Son Blanc.

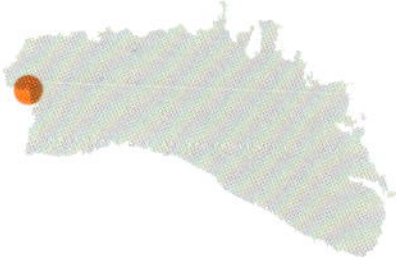

Cap d'Artrutx

Santandria | Cala Blanca | Cala en Bosc | Son Xoriguer

Santandria is a narrow and elongated inlet which has always been Ciutadella's traditional playground. It also played an important role in the 18th century when it became the gateway to the city under French domination.

Cala Blanca, further to the south, mixes the local atmosphere with the tourist scene, here more emphatic. There are prehistoric caves around both the coves.

At **Cap d'Artrutx**, the south-western extreme of the island, the land slopes gently down to the channel between Menorca and Mallorca. The Cap d'Artrutx and Capdepera lighthouses mark the coastlines of the respective islands.

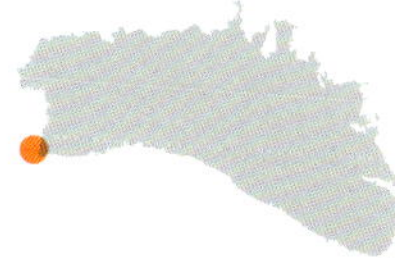

Cala en Bosc, the westernmost beach on the south coast, is surrounded today by holiday resorts of recent creation. An inland lagoon was beeen converted into that include an artificial inland lake where a pleasure harbour has been built.

The natural bay formed by **Son Xoriguer** beach marks the border between the holiday resort and the undeveloped open space, which is a bit further on.

Son Saura
Es Talaier | Cala en Turqueta

On Ciutadella's south coast, **Son Saura**, **Es Talaier**, **En Turqueta** and **Macarella** comprise an area that has, fortunately, been protected from development and whose beaches remain unspoilt. **Son Saura** is the largest of them.

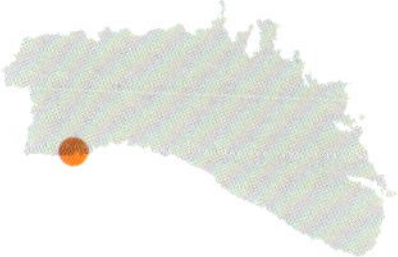

Beyond Son Saura and the Punta d'es Governador, **Es Talaier** is a delightful spot. As in the case of the neighbouring beaches, the decomposition of the limestone soil has created the white sand that is so characteristic of this area. (See excursion 17 page 83). This is one of the naturists favourite beaches.

On contemplating **Cala en Turqueta** (in this photo) and **Macarella-Macarelleta** (shown in the following double page spread) it is easy to see why these beaches are considered among the island's finest. On "peak" summer days bathers reach them by land and sea and they can become very crowded indeed.

Macarella | Macarelleta

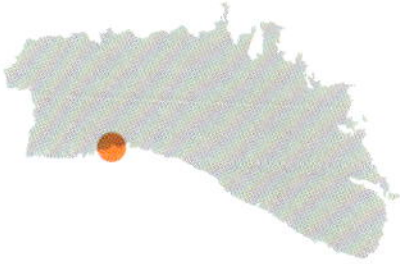

CALA GALDANA
CALA TREBALÚGER
SANT TOMÀS
SON BOU
CALA EN PORTER

Cova d'en Xoroi, at Cala en Porter

Cala Galdana

Cala Trebalúger

Binigaus beach

Cala Mitjaneta

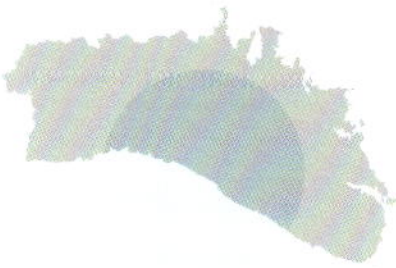

SOUTH

FROM **CALA GALDANA** TO **CALA EN PORTER**

Between the Algendar gorge that marks the boundary between the Ciutadella and Ferreries districts and the Cala en Porter gorge in Alaior, this central stretch of the southern coast is characterized by the streams and torrents that have cleaved their way through the limestone land surface on their way to the sea.

The coastline, fairly elevated at Cala Galdana, drops slowly until it reaches Binigaus, starting point of an almost uninterrupted stretch of some of the island's most popular sandy beaches: Sant Adeodat, Sant Tomàs, Atàlitx and Son Bou, whose eastern extreme is marked by the cliffs at Cap de Ses Penyes.

The limpid, calm waters of the beautiful Mitjana, Trebalúger, Fustam and Escorxada coves are the great attraction of this area and Cala Galdana, despite the impact of the tourist development that has taken place there, is still the most symbolic of the Menorcan coastline.

Groves of pine trees that grow down as far as the sandy beaches, emerald green waters, luxuriant vegetation and freshwater springs running down the gorges all combine to create an idyllic setting.

It is perhaps in this part of the island where the visitor encounters the widest and richest range of alternatives offered by nature: from long, open beaches packed with cosmopolitan tourists, easily reached from Ferreries, Es Migjorn or Alaior (see map and itineraries), to secluded coves only accessible by boat or on foot. There are hotels and appartments at Cala Galdana, St. Tomàs and Son Bou that offer all kinds of services and conveniences.

EXCURSIONS
BY FOOT
OR BY BICYCLE

SOUTH

FROM
CALA GALDANA
TO
CALA EN PORTER

18

Ferreries
Algendar gorge

19

Cala Galdana
Cala Trebalúger

20

Cave Na Polida
Cave Es Coloms

21

Sant Adeodat
Cala Escorxada
Cala Fustam

22

Es Migjorn
Binigaus

23

Sant Tomàs
Son Bou basilica

Son Picard
es Coster des Pastor
Biniat
Binisarret
Binisarraia
Binicreixent
Bellamirada de Dalt
Bellamirada Vella
Me-15
Me-7
Mota Gran
s'Albufera
Pujol Roig
94
Marina de Bellavista
Cànova Nova
Sant Josep
Montnegre
168
Estància de Montpalau
Estància de Barbatx
Barbatxí
Estància d'en Siano
Sant Joan de Carbonell
Sant Joan des Horts
Estància de Sant Diego
s'Hort de Llucatx
Coves Velles
Calòritx
Ruma Nou
Sant Pere
Montpalau
Barbatx
Son Servera
Llucatx
ses Coves Velles
es Caragol
Penya des Corb
Molinet
Estància de Calòritx
Binigurdó
190
Llucatx
sa Cimentera
Santa Rita
Llinàritx Nou
s'Alzina Grossa
Peu del Toro
l'Enzell
235
Son Làdico
ES MERCADAL
SA ROCA
Me-1
Llinàritx Vell
Me-13
el Toro
358
Mare de Déu del Toro
Puig de s'Ermità
238
Albaida
172
Binifabini
Son Arró Gran
Rafalet Nou
s'Atalaia
Son Arret
Rafal Roig
es Xalet
sa Farinera
Rafal des Frares
Santa Eulàlia de Dalt
Son Alzina
Roca des Frare
202
s'Arangí
Alcotx
Planes de s'Albaida
els Amaradors
sa Granada de Dalt
Binifailla
Puig Mal
214
s'Aranjassa
Me-9
Son Vidal
sa Granada de Baix
Puig Mal
Binillubet
Estància d'en Rovella
s'Albaida
Font Redona
238
Biniatzem
Binissegui
Estància de Binillubet
Santa Eularieta
Son Gall
es Pi
Me-18
Font Redona de Baix
Font Redona de Dalt
Sant Jeroni
Estància d'en Nofre
Estància Cucanya
Son Puig
Santa Bàrbara
Son Benet
Sant Joan
s'Artiga Vella
Son Trèmol
Hort de Son Trèmol
Me-16
Estància de Sant Josep
Estància des Borinot
s'Artigueta
Camp Siquiat
Son Planes
ES MIGJORN GRAN
es Bec Nou
es Bec Vell
Turmaden
Sant Josep
Estància Camí del Toro
Son Roca
es Camp Siquiat
Riu de la Plata
Me-1
Biniguarda Vell
Estància de Binixebonet
Biniguarda Nou
Biniatzau
Son Pons
es Becs
Santa Creu
s'Almudaina
Llimpet
Son Bonaventura
Rafal Fort
Biniguarda
es Cos
Borrassos Nou
Sant Miquel
22
Son Torres
la Cova
Llimpa
Son Blanc Vell
Binixebó
Santa Clara
Barranc de Binigaus
Santa Mònica
es Barranquet
Binixebonet
Santa Magdalena
ALAIOR
LA TROTXA
Santa Mònica
Santa Catalina
Vil·la Tanús
Me-18
Santa Ponça
Llumena Nou
Deià Vell
Son Blanc Nou
sa Mola
es Llumenes
Son Saura
Santa Ponça
Borrassos Vell
Santa Mariana
Sant Agustí de na Polida
Terres Noves
Son Seren
Llumena
Lloc Nou de Mestre
Son Pinaret
Santa Victòria
Son Pons
Llucassaldent Major
s'Albegall
Santa Anna des Rafal
Son Fabiol
Sant Tomàs
ses Cuques
sa Vall
Estància d'en Cavaller
Biniarbolla
Rafal Nou
L'ARGENTINA
SANT TOMÀS
136
Son Cart
Binifamis
Biniac-Argentina
Torre Solí Vell
Rafalet
Torralba Petit
Torralba
23
Can Llopis
Llogaret
Binicalsitx
Torralba den Salord
Sant Benet
Binialmés
Son Cartet
Estància de Llucassaldent
Son Mannà
Torre Solí Nou
TORRE SOLÍ
Torralbet
ses Canessies
es Taronger
Torralba Nou
Talis
SANT JAUME MEDITERRANI
Estància de Son Mannà
Torre Vella
Llucalari Vell
Son Bou
Santa Cecília
Son Segui
Sant Jaume
Sant Tomàs
Torre d'en Galmés
Binialmaia
Platja de Sant Tomàs
Punta de Talis
SON BOU
LLUCALARI
Estància d'en Carreres
Biniarroi
Punta Rodona
Torre d'en Galmés
Binigemor
Llucalari Nou
Son Vidal
Platges de Son Bou
Biniarroiet
Llucalari de Sant Antoni
Cotaina
Basílica de Son Bou
ses Roques Llises
Son Domingo
Son Sanxo
Son Alberti
Sant Bartomeu
Son Costes
Sant Llorenç
GR 223
Torre Llissà Nou
Torrellisar Vell
Torre Vella
Torrellisar Vell
Hort d'Alcaidús
Ca'n Rabassó
Cap de ses Penyes
Caleta de Llucalari
Cova de sa Calç
Son Esquella
Hort de Biniarroiet
Torralbenc Vell
Torralbenc Nou
So na Caçana
So na Caçana
Santa Cristina
Penyes d'Alaior
Binissagarra
Biniadrix
Lloc Nou
Me-12
Biniadrix de Dalt
Binicalaf Vell
Fita de sa Torre Vella
Biniadrix de Baix
Punta de Sant Llorenç
Caleta de Sant Llorenç
es Prat
Barranc de Cala en Porter
sa Torre Nova
Sant Eloi
BINIXICA
CALA EN PORTER
CALES COVES
SON VITAMINA
Son Frau
Roca de s'Aigua
Racó de sa Talaia
Llenegall de s'Aigua
Morro Esclafat
Cala en Porter
Cales Coves
Binicalaf Nou
Cova d'en Xoroi
Cova de Sant Josep
Morro de Ponent
Cales Coves
Morro de Llevant
na Blanca
es Maresosa
na Mala
na Calenta
ES CANUTELLS
Caparrot de Forma

Algendar gorge

Cala Mitjana

Cave Es Coloms

18

Ferreries Algendar gorge

This is another way to visit the lovely **Algendar gorge** (see itinerary 15 on page 83). At the roundabout of Ferreries you must take the turning signposted as Barranc d'Algendar, and drive steeply uphill along the asphalted road which, owing to its elevation, offers good views of **S'Enclusa** to the north. Turning then in a southerly direction towards the coast, it will lead us to **Es Canaló**, where we must leave the car and continue on foot down to the river-bed. Here, we will notice a radical change in the vegetation as we penetrate the micro-climate of the gorge, where palm and fruit-trees, lianas and ferns grow in almost tropical profusion. Crossing the river-bed, if we have arranged for return transport, we can join the previously mentioned itinerary, in the opposite direction.

—

Time approx.: 1h (return) for the part on foot

19

Cala Galdana Cala Trebalúger

The path starts in the high part of the urbanisation and after going through pine woods reaches **Cala Mitjana** and then **Trebalúger**. If one feels up to a longer walk, it is possible to link up with itinerary 22 and finish at the beach of **Sant Adeodat**.

—

Time approx.: 3h (return)

20

Cave Na Polida Cave Es Coloms

To reach these interesting caves we must leave the car park at **Sant Adeodat** and walk to **Binigaus** beach where, near the middle, a path leads us towards the gorge. After about three hundred metres, we leave the main river-bed to the left, climb a wall and follow the left bank of the stream for about half a kilometre. Here, we take the fork that takes us over to the other side to the **Na Polida** cave where, with the aid of a torch, we will see extraordinary marble-like stalactites which, unfortunately, show clear signs of vandalism. From here we return to the left bank and, about half a kilometre further up, crossing back to the right, we reach the **Es Coloms** cave, also known as Sa Catedral owing to its size: the oval-shaped entrance is 24 metres high.

—

Time approx.: 2h 30m (return)

Sant Adeodat beach

21

Sant Adeodat Cala Escorxada Cala Fustam

In the first section the walk goes along the beach-es of **Binigaus**. At the end of these, it enters the pine wood and takes us to **Escorxada** and **Fustam**.See Itinerary 22 as an alterna-tive in the other direction.

—

Time approx.: 2h 30m (return)

Binigaus

22

Es Migjorn Binigaus

This alternative route to **Binigaus** beach is, in itself, a pleasant walk, particularly the last stretch that takes us along the gorge, with fine scenery. .

—

Time approx.: 1h 30m (return)

Son Bou basilica

23

Sant Tomàs Son Bou basilica

From one end to the other of both beaches, a path takes us along the coast, this is an interesting walk for those who are bored with just ly-ing in the sun. From **Punta de Talis** there is a good view of **Son Bou** and, at the end, we may visit the remains of the early-Christian basilica.

—

Time approx.: 2h 30m (return)

From **Talis**, view inland of the island, with **El Toro** in the background and the point of **Na Rodona** in the foreground.

Cala Galdana

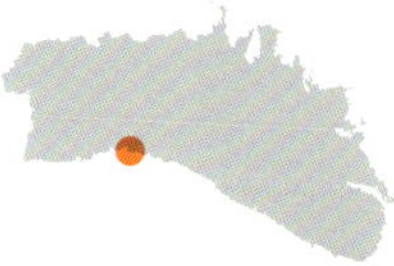

Cala Galdana is a name that rings out in the hearts of all those who really love Menorca. It is in a wonderful, spectacular setting where the flora and fauna of the gorges has survived intact. The majority of the high areas are covered with dense pinewoods, and the perfect line of the beach makes one ask if it is in fact real.

In the first of these images, you can clearly appreciate the navigable mouth of the ravines of **Algendar** and **Algendaret**. In the latter, the large hotel stands out scandalously, attached to the cliff, built in the first years of its urbanistic development

Trebalúger

Cala Mitjana | Cala Fustam | Cala Escorxada

The following four photographs offer an overall impression of the south coast beaches. Lying at the outlets of the successive gorges that cross the hinterland, they are invariably surrounded by pinewoods and the colour and transparency of the water, as seen here in **Cala Mitjana**, cannot be matched elsewhere.

The fertile soil of the **Sa Cova** gorge(or Son Fideu) is exploited for vegetable and fruit farming before it reaches the sea. At the mouth of the gorge, **Trebalúger**, although a popular beach in summer, remains unspoilt thanks to its difficult access by car.

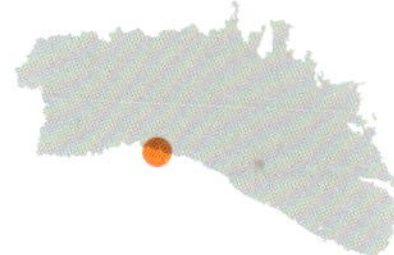

Another view of **Trebalúger** clearly shows how the beach acts as a separation between the sea and the approaching stream which rarely flows large enough to overcome this natural barrier. (See excursion 20 on page 102).

Although **Fustam** and **Escorxada** are separated by the Punta de Sant Antoni, the distance between them is so short that they are generally considered as a whole. The photo clearly shows the richness of the pinewoods and excellent state of conservation in all these coves more than justifies their qualification as protected areas. (See excursion 22, page 103).

Son Bou
Binigaus | Sant Tomàs | Talis

In the central part of the south coast, the characteristic configuration of gorges and coves changes as the cliffs give way to a more gently sloping seaboard. Beyond **Binigaus**, between the alluvial farmland and the sea, dunes are formed.

After the rocks of Codrell we come to the beaches of **Sant Adeodat** and **Sant Tomàs**, a developed sector with hotels and apartments. This wide perspective remind us that we are on an island.

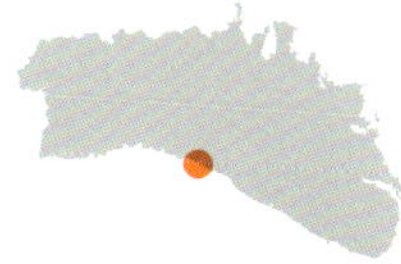

Good panoramic views of Son Bou can be seen from the **Punta d'Atàlitx**. Behind the fields is a pinewood that provides us with the only shade around when the sun is beating down. At this point the beach is at its narrowest but, as it is also more secluded, it is a popular spot with nudists.

Son Bou is the island's longest beach (nearly 4 km) and also the most crowded. Its size and the tourist attractions (including an aquatic park) found near the hotels make it an ideal beach for children. At the far end, an early Christian basilica can be visited.

Son Bou

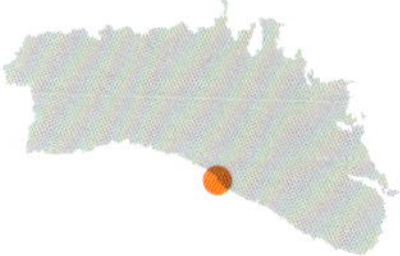

Cala en Porter
Cala Sant Llorenç | Sa Torre Nova

Beyond Cap de Ses Penyes that limits Son Bou to the east, the coastline again tends towards tiny coves set among cliffs, such as **Sant Llorenç** that marks the outlet of the Torre Vella gorge.

While man struggles to make the most of the shallow soil of the clifftop, far below, the sea erodes the foundations of the massive limestone block. To the left, the ruins of the **Torre Nova** watchtower bear witness to past concerns for pirate raids.

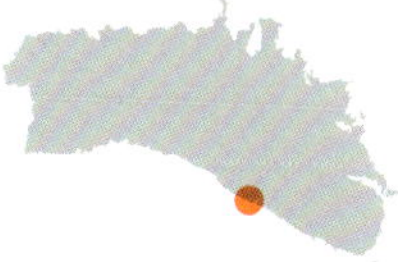

It is one of the island's larger beaches, **Cala en Porter** was among the first to undergo tourist development. On the cliff face, a natural cave, **Cova d'en Xoroi**, has been converted into a discotheque and offers spectacular views of the surrounding coast.

Menorca can be unmistakably identified from the air by the geometrical shapes formed by the dry-stone walls that form one of the island's most characteristic features.

CALESCOVES
CALA DES CANUTELLS
CALA BINIBÈQUER
PUNTA PRIMA
ALCALFAR

Cala Rafalet

Binibèquer beach

Biniancolla

Binibèquer Vell

SOUTHEAST

FROM **CALESCOVES** TO **CALA SANT ESTEVE**

Illa de l'Aire lighthouse

This area is confined by, on one side, the Cala en Porter gorge that descends from Alaior to the sea and, on the other, by an imaginary line drawn from the innermost extreme of Maó harbour to Alaior. It is a varied landscape, although generally flat and sparsely vegetated except for the occasional area of woodland near the coast. During the winter months when rainfall tends to be high, the landscape is covered by a lush, green blanket, but the rest of the year, the twisted, dry branches of the wild olive are the most apparent element. In the gently sloping areas closer to the coast, however, the vegetation is more typically Mediterranean with pines and the occasional evergreen oak.

Calescoves, Es Canutells, Binidalí and Biniparratx are examples of coves protected from the sea by high cliffs. From Binisafúller to Punta Prima, the coastline is less elevated but equally rocky. Punta Prima, the longest of these beaches, faces the Illa del Aire. From here as far as Cala Sant Esteve, before reaching the port of Maó, the east coast sees the sun rise from high cliffs with hardly any interruptions, except for Cala Alcalfar, S'Algar and Rafalet.

Of this coastline, the longest contour belongs to the town of Sant Lluís, including many property developments and some country houses of cultural and tourist interest

An interesting section of the Camí de Cavalls, an ancient coastal path, is that which goes between Punta Prima and Alcalfar.

EXCURSIONS
BY FOOT
OR BY BICYCLE

SOUTHEAST

FROM
CALESCOVES
TO
CALA SANT ESTEVE

24

Calescoves

25

Canutells
Caparrot de Forma

26

Sant Climent
Camí de Cotaina
Torrellisar Vell

27

Punta Prima
Rafalet gorge

28

Sant Lluís
Llucmaçanes
and hamlets

0
N
1
1 km
Cap de Mestral
Illa d'en Colom
Cap de LLevant
Cala de sa Torreta
sa Torreta
Torre Blanca
Turdonell de Dalt
Torre de Rambla
Cala des Tamarells
saTorre Blanca
Parc Natural
Estància des Prat
es Prat
sa Sella
Escola
sa Boal Vella
Santa Mariana
Ermita de Fàtima
Punta Fra Bernat
Platja des Grau
Illots de sa Cudia
Es Grau
Punta de sa Cudia
sa Cudia Nova
Punta de sa Galera
s'Albufera
s'Albufera
sa Boal Nova
s'Hort Nou
sa Boaleta
S'Albufera des Grau
sa Bassa
Pont Modorro
es Palmer
es Palmer Vell
es Palmer Nou
Sant Simó
Sant Ramon
sa Cudia Vella
es Violar
ses Salvatges Primes
Caló de ses Mandries
Cala Grau
ses Salvatges Fondes
Caleta de Binillautí
s'Esqueller
es Planàs
Son Cardona
ses Piquetes
Palafanguer de Baix
Son Mir
Milà Nou
GR 223
Macar de Binillautí
en Bombarda
Binillautí Nou
Estància de Milà
na Bona
Milà Vell
s' Esquena d'Ase
Binillautí Vell
Palafanguer de sa Barrera
Rafal Nou
es Milà
Binillautí
sa Raconada Vella
es Pa Gros
Binarroga
Rafal Vell
Me-5
Milà
92
Illots de sa Mesquida
Biniaixa
Algarrova
Serra Morena
Torre de sa Mesquida
Cala Mesquida
Sa Mesquida
Punta de sa Bateria Vella
Son Pons
Llibertó Vell
Algarrovet
Albiauet
Agotars
Sant Isidre
Punta Negre
es Murtar
Cala es Murtar
Rafal Colom
es Barranc de Biniai
Binisarmenya
Cap Negre
sa Granja
Pla dels Vergers
Me-3
Alfavaret
Sant Antoni
els Escullots
Talatí de Baix Nou
Son Petit
Sant Joan dels Vergers
sa Colàrsega
Cala Rata
Cala Llonga
ses Àligues
Cala Figuera
Maó
Son Cardona Nou
Curniola
el Fonduco
Punta de ses Bancades
Torelló d'en Mir
Cornia
es Fornàs
Me-2
RM
Son Vilar
Horizonte
es Castell
es Freus
Torelló Vell
na Ferranda
Robadones
Son Tudurí
Trepucó
sa Cúdia Cremada
sa Casa Nova
Illa del Llatzeret
la Mare de Déu
la Mola
la Mola
Punta de s'Esperó
72
Santa Ana
Me-12
Santa Margarida
PR ME2
Son Granot
Sol del Este
Mussupta de Baix
Malbúger Vell
s' Ereta
Santa Cecília
Son Biaü
Noria Riera
Punta de na Nega James
Climent
Llucmaçanes
Me-14
Me-8
Son Amat
es Clot
Bintaufa Vell
na Xenxa d'en Borràs
Cf-2
Aeroclub de Sant Lluís
Torre Vella
Castell de Sant Felip
Punta de Sant Carles
Me-6
Cala Sant Esteve
Joraixa des Pi
Fort Malborough
Hipòdrom
Son Tretze Nou
Biniarroca
Poligon Industrial
Sant Antoni Verd
Sant Llorenç
Sant Joan de Binissaida
s'Esbrufador
Aeroport de Menorca
Santa Catalina
Toraixa de sa Figuera
ses Aubertones
Baix d'en Jaume
Biniparrell
Trebalúger
ses Cometes
Binissaida
Caló des Vi Blanc
Moli de Dalt
Trebalugeret
Trebalúger
na Girada
sa Cigonya
sa Parereta
Santa Rita
Pou Nou
Son Vidal
Binisafúller d'en Cardona
Binisafuet
Sant Lluís
Rafalet Petit
Rafaletó
Rafalet Vell
Rafalet Nou
es Sòtil
Binisafúller de Baix
S'Ullastrar
28
So n'Aritja
Son Bonaventura
es Rafalet
es Niu de Falcons
Biniali
Me-10
es Consell
Torret
es Camp Sarc
s'Olivera
Barranc des Rafalet
Caló des Rafalet
Binibèquer Vell
So n'Abatzer
Costa des Còdol
Biniancolla
Me-8
S'Algar
Binisafúller Nou
Binisafúller de sa Torre
Alcalfar Nou
Alcalfar Vell
Punta Rafalet
s'Algar
Santa Rosa
Alcalfar
Binibèquer Nou
Alcalfar de sa Cala
Cala d'Alcalfar
Morro d'Alcalfar
Torre d'Alcalfar
Binibèquer
Torret
Torret de Baix
Binibequer Vell
73
Racó des Llexiu
sa Serreta
Torret de Baix
Son Remei
27
GR 223
na Foradada
Biniancolla
Son Ganxo
Punta dels Mabres
Platja de Punta Prima
Punta Prima
Cala de Binibèquer
Torre Son Ganxo
Costa d'en Sivineta
Caló Fondo
Cap d'en Botifarra
Caló d'en Fust
Caló d'en Morla
Racó d'en Bruixa
Caló de S'Olli
Cala de Biniancolla
Punta des Milans
Illot des Cagaire
es Moll
Cap de Llevant
Illa de l'Aire

Calescoves

Caparrot de Forma

24

Calescoves

Turn off the Sant Climent-Cala en Porter road at the Son Vitamina urbanisation, leave the car in the new stretch of road and walk down towards the sea. The cliffs that overlook the peaceful waters of the double cove are dotted with troglodyte burial caves. The whole necropolis has been declared a National Historic and Artistic Monument and steps are being taken to bring it up to standard.

—

Time approx.: 1h (return)

25

Canutells
Caparrot de Forma

On reaching the road to **Cala Canutells**, turn left in the direction of the coast, at the entrance to the urbanisation. You can leave the vehicle at the end of Carrer Forma. From here, a short walk will lead us along the cliff to the **Caparrot de Forma** headland, from where we will see the neighbouring troglodyte caves and from right to left, an extensive view of the south coast.

—

Time approx.: 30m (return)

Cotaina estate

26

Sant Climent Camí de Cotaina Torrellisar Vell

This excursion brings us into contact with the characteristic landscape and architecture of rural Menorca in an area where few transformations have taken place over the years. Leaving from **Sant Climent** you must reach the houses of Algendar and turn left, along the Camí de Sa Serra, and follow the gently sloping hill past the Son Orfila and Montper farmhouses to **Cotaina**. When we reach the Alaior-Cala en Porter road, we drive across and continue to the **Torrellisar Vell** farm where a signpost indicates an unusual *taula*. Leave the car on the way and continue walking in order not to bother the farm work.

Rafalet gorge

27

Punta Prima Rafalet gorge

From the left end of the beach, looking towards the sea, you must follow the coast along the Camí de Cavalls until the old **Torre d'Alcalfar** and **Caló Roig**, enjoying lovely views of **Illa de l'Aire** and its lighthouse along the way. **Alcalfar** will soon come in to sight, with its houses clustered round the bay and protective rocky headland of Es Torn. On the main Sant Lluís road we reencounter the pathway that will take us right across the **S'Algar** urbanisation access road. We follow this unmade track, beyond the last houses, to the gorge, and descend through the welcome shade of the dense woodland between abrupt cliff faces to the diminutive cove for a refreshing swim.

—

Time approx.: 3h (return)

Llucmaçanes church

28

Sant Lluís, Llucmaçanes and hamlets

We leave Sant Lluís on the Punta Prima road and take the first turning to the right which will lead us to the picturesque hamlet of **Torret**, carefully conserved on the outside. We cross the hamlet until the main **Binibèquer-Binisafúller** road where we turn left through **S'Ullastrar** as far as the talayot of **Binisafuet** with the *talaiot*, a small *taula* and other remains of the settlement. Here we turn right and continue beyond Sa Parereta (a restaurant) where we take another right turn to follow the old Volta des Milord (His Lordship's Walk), as far as the Biniparrell junction where we turn left towards **Llucmaçanes**. As high dry-stone walls flank both sides of the road during much of this circuit, better visibility will be enjoyed by bicycle than by car. If we do not wish to return via Sant Lluís, there are two accesses to the main Maó-airport road.

The **Cala en Porter** gorge is the western border of the area described below. In the foreground we can see the steps and the terraces of **Cova d'en Xoroi** in the wall of the cliffs.

Calescoves

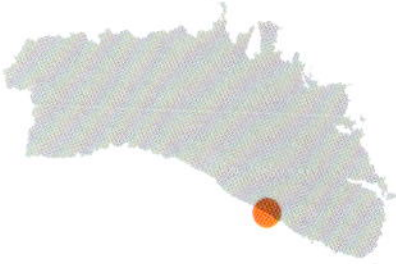

The name of **Calescoves** is derived from the many caves excavated in the cliff walls in prehistoric times. There is evidence that they were burial places but, in recent times, they have been used as living accommodation. The shelter afforded by this double cove means that it is usually replete with pleasure craft. (See excursion 24, page 118).

Canutells
Caparrot de Forma | Binidalí

Cala Canutells has grown spectacularly. People from Sant Climent and Maó were, at one time, the only visitors, but the small and protected beach has undergone great change in recent years and its family atmosphere is disappearing.

From the sea, many caves are visible on the cliff faces where wild birds make their nests, among them sea birds and wild pigeons.

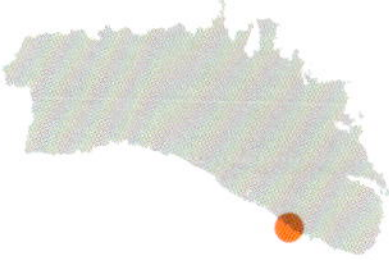

The headland to the west of **Binidalí** is another excellent viewpoint over this stretch of the coastline. Although the entrance to the cove is quite ample, the beach is diminutive but many natural platforms exist in the surrounding rocks for sunbathing or diving.

Binibèquer

Biniparratx | Cap d'en Font | Binisafúller

At **Biniparratx**, the inlet describes a marked angle between the high cliff walls making it an ideal refuge for boats in bad weather. Here, too, prehistoric caves can be seen at its innermost extreme similar to those at Calescoves.

Beyond **Cap d'en Font**, the coastline of the Sant Lluís area appears as an unbroken chain of developments and resorts. Just a few years ago, the cove at **Binisafúller** (in the foreground) comprised of no more than a few traditional weekend houses, now surrounded by modern villas.

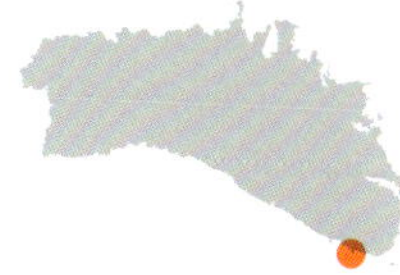

The "fishermen's village" at **Binibèquer Vell** is one of the most visited tourist settings. Its curious construction aims to reproduce the style and use of raw materials typical of popular Mediterranean architecture.

Binibèquer, just beyond the aforementioned village, is a beach of fine sand protected from the wind by the Morro d'en Xuia headland. The following inlet is **Cala Torret**, surrounded by the resort of the same name.

Binibèquer

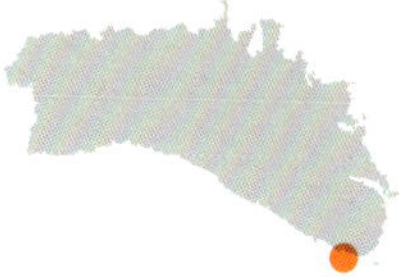

Punta Prima
Biniancolla | Illa de l'Aire | Alcalfar

Biniancolla is the last of the south-facing coves. The oldest of the houses stand, literally, in the water and their ground floors are used as boathouses.

Punta Prima was appropriately named Sandy Bay by the British during their domination of the island. Always a popular holiday spot among Menorcans, the resort has grown following the building of a large hotel. Recent work is bringing the roads and services of the resort up to standard.

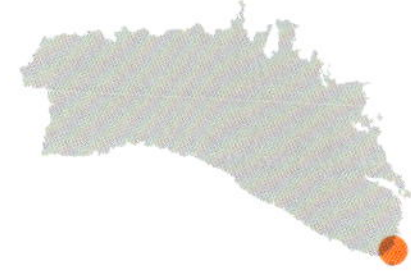

The **Illa del Aire** which rises no more than 15m above sea-level at its highest point near the lighthouse, is unique in many ways, one of them as the home to a subspecies of endemic black lizards.

Dominating the cove, the spectacular **watch tower** adds a special force to the simple landscape.

Cala Rafalet
S'Algar | Cala Sant Esteve

S'Algar is a traditional resort situated on a rocky headland eroded by the sea. The absence of a beach is more than made up for by the many facilities available to the visitor. The tiny Cala Rafalet lies just beyond, hidden by the high cliffs.

Although the cove of **Cala Rafalet** affords barely enough space to spread out a couple of beach towels, the beauty of the grove of holm oaks through which one passes on the way to the sea, and the views over the cliffs, more than warrant the walk.

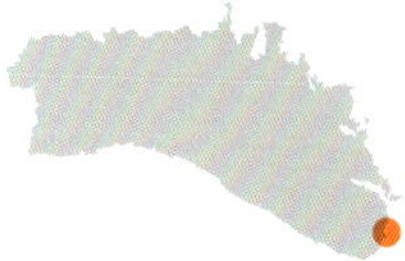

Cala Sant Esteve is surrounded by the military fortifications that speak to us of Menorca's turbulent history. The recently renovated Fort Marlborough (to the right) can be visited as can the military museum that stands in what remains of the legendary Castell de Sant Felip.

Returning to our starting point, the old fortress of **La Mola de Maó** overshadows the southernmost headland of the south coast. Its location has lost the strategic importance of times gone by, and today is a much-visited monument which appears to peaceably stand guard over Menorca and all her treasures.

CAR TOURS

1
FROM **MAÓ**
TO **SON PARC**

2
FROM **ALAIOR**
TO **CAP DE CAVALLERIA**

3
AROUND
CIUTADELLA

4
SOUTHEASTERN
AREA

5
FROM
ES MERCADAL
TO **CALA GALDANA**

Conventional signs

- Lighthouse
- Defence tower
- Beaches
- Panoramic view
- Commercial harbour
- Recreational harbour
- Fishing harbour
- Quarries of marès
- Mill
- Old chapel, church
- Camping
- Filling station
- Airport
- Aerodrome
- Talaiotic settlement
- Taula
- Talaiot
- Naveta
- Caves
- Early-christian basilica
- Main road
- Secondary road
- Paved track
- Urbanization road
- Unmade track
- Narrow path
- Brook
- Camí de Cavalls

Illa des Porros
Cap de Cavalleria
Port de Sanitja
sa Talaia
Sanitja
Illes Bledes
Cala Barril
Cala Pregonda
Platja de Binimel·là
Platja de Cavalleria
Platja de Farragut
Cala Mica
Cap de Fornells
Cala Tirant
Torre de Fornells
Fornells
Badia de Fornells
ses Salines
Arenal de Son Saura
Arenal d'en Castell
Son Parc
Punta Grossa
Arenal d'en Castell
na Macaret
Illa Petita de Addaia
Illa Gran de Addaia
Coves Noves
Addaia
Port d'Addaia
Sant Joan des Horts
es Mercadal
sa Roca
Mare de Déu del Toro
Cap de Favàritx
Platja d'en Tortuga
Ferreries
Son Mercer de Dalt
sa Torre Blanca
Cala de sa Torreta
Illa d'en Colom
Sant Llorenç de Binixems
Ermita de Fàtima
Platja des Grau
s'Albufera
es Grau
es Migjorn Gran
Binicodrell
Santa Mònica
Cova des Coloms
Sant Agustí
Cova de na Pulida
Sant Tomàs
Alaior
Santa Ponça
sa Mola
la Argentina
Rafal Rubí
Torralba
Torre Soli
San Jaume
Son Bou
Basílica de Son Bou
Llucalari
Torre d'en Galmés
ses Roques Llises
Serra Morena
sa Mesquida
Cala Mesquida
Cala es Murtar
es Murtar
Sant Antoni
Cap Negre
Cala Llonga
Punta de s'Esperó
La Mola
Sant Joan dels Vergers
Talatí de Dalt
Torre Llissà
So na Caçana
Curnia
Maó
es Castell
Torelló
es Fornàs
Sant Climent
Robadones
Trepucó
Sol del Este
Castell de Sant Felip
Cala Sant Esteve
Fort Malborough
Torre d'en Penjat
sa Torre Nova
Cales Coves
Binixica
Llucmassanes
Son Vitamina
Cala en Porter
Aeroport de Menorca
Sant Lluís
Trebalúger
Binisafuet
S'Ullastrar
Caló des Rafalet
Caparrot de Forma
Binidalí
Biniparratx
Cap d'en Font
Torret
Alcaufar
s'Algar
Alcalfar
Cala d'Alcalfar
Binibeca Vell
Torret de Baix
Biniancolla
Son Ganxo
Punta Prima
Platja de Punta Prima
Illa d'el Aire
Platja de Binigaus
Platja de Sant Adeodat
Platja de Sant Tomàs
Platges de Son Bou
Cala en Porter
Cova d'en Xoroi
Cales Coves
es Canutells
Cala de Binidalí
Cala de Biniparratx
Cap d'en Font
Cala de Binisafúller
Cala de Biniancolla
ME-1
ME-20
ME-18
ME-16
ME-15
ME-13
ME-7
ME-11
ME-5
ME-3
ME-2
ME-12
ME-14
ME-8
ME-6
ME-10
CF-3

Isabel II Fortress, La Mola

FROM **MAÓ** TO **SON PARC**

- LA MOLA
- CALA MESQUIDA
- ES GRAU
- FAVÀRITX
- PORT D'ADDAIA
- NA MACARET
- ARENAL D'EN CASTELL
- SON PARC

Starting from the innermost extreme of the port, **Sa Colàrsega**, to reach the Isabel II Fortress, on **La Mola**, we take the Me-3 road, passing behind the power station and naval base, above the villas in Cala Rata and Cala Sant Antoni and close by the colonial-style **Golden Farm**, allegedly a temporary residence of Lord Nelson. Its colonial-style façade, painted in the typical "English red" can be best seen from the other side of the port, whereas from here or from the neighbouring **Cala Llonga** resort, we can enjoy splendid views of the city of Maó and Es Castell.Further on, we arrive at La Mola, the fortress built during the reign of Isabel II to take the place of the demolished Castell de Sant Felip which had stood on the opposite shore. A visit to the complex is very interesting.

From this point, the **Els Freus** isthmus, we can see the walled precinct of El Llatzaret, which became an island in 1900 as a result of the opening of the Alfons XII, or Sant Jordi, Canal. We will have a better view of El Llatzaret when we retrace our steps towards the Cala Mesquida junction where we will turn right. We are on some hills carpeted by low and resistant vegetation where some say the best camomile in Menorca can be picked.

Cala Mesquida is a nucleus of traditional holiday houses and jetties clustered around the little **Sa Raconada** bay with Sa Mesquida beach just beyond and an 18th century

S'Albufera des Grau

Favàritx lighthouse

Arenal de s'Olla (Son Parc)

watchtower overlooking from above. From here, we return to Maó and start the second phase of our tour by taking the Me-5 road towards **Es Grau**.

This road diverts from the Me-7 Fornells road just beyond the **Pla dels Vergers**, or Pla de Sant Joan, vegetable gardens, which we pass on our left, and travels northwards through uneven terrain right up to the beach and village of **Es Grau** from where we may choose to take a boat trip over to **Illa d'En Colom**, at the edge of the bay. **S'Albufera**, a sea-water lagoon of notable interest to biologists and naturalists, is another point of notable interest (see excursion 2 on page 44). To continue our tour, we must return to the junction with the Me-7 road and follow it 8 km to the Hermitage of Fàtima.

About 500 metres beyond, we turn right on the Cf-1 road, as if following the direction indicated by a curiously shaped craggy rock known as **Sa Sella** (the saddle), that stands alone in the middle of the plain. At the end of this road we come to **Cap de Favàritx** and the lighthouse of the same name. The last stretch is in rather poor condition, but the unusual, almost lunar landscape of black slate, eroded by the sea for millennia, more than makes up for the uncomfortable drive.

You can reach the superb beaches of Presili and Tortuga, to the south of this point, on foot along a path without asphalt. We return again to the PM-710 road and after about fifteen km take the turning to the right which leads us, first to **Port d'Addaia**, a long, narrow bay that penetrates more than three km. inland through a richly wooded area, **Na Macaret** where many people from Alaior have their holiday homes and boathouses and, finally, the beach and modern urbanisation of **Arenal d'en Castell** with its hotels and more recent tourist developments.

Son Parc is the next place to be visited. An important tourist centre, here Menorca's only golf course is to be found along with various complexes of apartments and villas which surround the magnificent beach of **Son Saura del Nord**, or Arenal de S'Olla. To round off our tour, we will return to Maó by an alternative route, turning right at the Na Macaret-Addaia junction along the **Camí Vell d'Alaior** which leads us to the **Camí d'en Kane**. This drive offers the chance to appreciate the marked differences between the coast and the rural inland scenery of luxuriant woods of pines and evergreen oaks, farmsteads and old mansions scattered along the final stretch.

Binimel·là

FROM **ALAIOR** TO **CAP DE CAVALLERIA**

- EL TORO
- BINIMEL·LÀ
- PREGONDA
- CAVALLERIA
- CALA TIRANT
- FORNELLS
- SA ROCA

Our starting point is the higher part of the town of Alaior where the **Camí d'en Kane** (reconstructed and paved) passes by the cemetery and then leads towards **Es Mercadal**. We pass through some woody areas and cross the **Pla d'Alaior** with its curious rock formations that stand out in the flat landscape, basically dedicated to cattle farming, with **El Toro** soon appearing ahead of us.

On arrival at Es Mercadal we start the climb that winds its way up to the top of El Toro, Menorca's highest geographical point. From here we can enjoy a complete view of the surrounding island and visit the hermitage dedicated to **Our Lady of the Toro**, the patron saint of Menorca.

We return to Es Mercadal and, ignoring the signposts to Fornells, look for the sign that reads Platges Costa Nord (north coast beaches) which will lead us to the **Camí de Tramuntana**. This road takes us through an important agricultural area and, following the contours of the hills, offers wider, more panoramic views than is usual on the island. Generally, visibility from the roads is limited by the ever-present dry-stone walls. This is an interesting drive at any time of year, each season bringing with it a new colour scheme.

The direction we are in and the new signposts mean we cannot get lost: we follow the road towards **Binimel·là** and **Pregonda**; the

Cala Pregonda

Fornells port

latter cove, known as the pearl of the north coast, should only be visited if we have plenty of time, because reaching it is difficult and must be on foot (see excursion 10 on page 65). Binimel·là in itself is well worth the trip and we can have a swim and a drink in the beach bar.

Our next destination is **Cap de Cavalleria**, perhaps the island's most impressive scenario where the effect of the notorious tramuntana, or north wind, is most manifest. The lighthouse stands on a rocky headland where goats subsist on the few sparse shrubs that manage to survive in such inhospitable terrain. It is a sheer ninety metre drop to the sea below. From the cliff-top the views of the coast are most spectacular.On the way back from the lighthouse, on the right-hand side of the road, lays the little port of **Sanitja**, site of first, Phoenician, and then Roman settlements. The remains of an early Christian basilica are to be found near the watchtower on the Es Brau headland opposite.

We will now head towards Fornells, maybe stopping on the way to visit the rapidly developing tourist centre of **Cala Tirant** and the marshland zone which lies just inland. **Fornells** is the safest port to be found on the rugged north coast and, as such, is invariably packed with boats, and the ample bay is ideal for windsurfing. Owing to the rapid growth of tourism, Fornells has been transformed from a sleepy fishing village to a busy, cosmopolitan town. Nevertheless, it retains much of its picturesque charm and offers pleasant strolls through the old streets or out along the quay where a watchtower dating from the British occupation still stands. No visit to Fornells is complete without trying the famous *caldereta de llagosta* (lobster stew) at one of the many palm-tree-lined waterfront restaurants.

Leaving Fornells on the Me-15 towards Es Mercadal, we then turn off on the Me-7 towards Maó until we reach the junction with the access road to the **Sa Roca** urbanisation. This road will lead us back to Alaior, passing through woodlands and the Hermitage of Santa Ester on the way.

Cala Morell

AROUND DE **CIUTADELLA**

- **PUNTA NATI**
- **CALA MORELL**
- **ALGAIARENS**
- **CAP D'ARTRUTX**
- **SON SAURA**
- **SANT JOAN DE MISSA**
- **CALA EN TURQUETA**
- **CALA MACARELLA**
- **NAVETA DES TUDONS**

From Ciutadella it is impossible to visit the three neighbouring coastal areas without repeatedly returning to the city as no circular road exists. Several separate excursions are therefore necessary.

The first starts at the Sa Font bastion from where we take the Cf-5 to **Punta Nati.** The trip is well worth making as it takes us through some interesting countryside. After a few cultivated plots of land, the landscape becomes quite desolate and beyond the Torre Vella estate, where various talayots are found, there is nothing but stone as far as the eye can see.

The lighthouse, with a few surrounding bunkers, overlooks the rugged coastline, infamous for the many shipwrecks that have taken place here through the centuries. Here, Egyptian vultures, a bird of prey now extinct on the rest of the islands, can still be seen flying overhead and another curiosity of the area are *ponts*, strange stone constructions built as shelters for livestock. Just before the lighthouse there is a particularly notable, seven-tiered pont with a perfectly formed vault inside. Engraved in the stone, the builder's name and the date, 1857.

For our second tour, we leave Ciutadella's industrial estate on the road to **Cala Morell** and **Algaiarens**, the old Camí de la Vall. Along the first stretch of the road, what were once modest constructions for storing farming implements have been converted into chalets

Pont near Punta Nati

Cala en Turqueta

with vegetable gardens and orchards. We are in the area of big estates where ahead we see the fortified tower of **Torre d'en Quart**, after which we must take the road to the **Cala Morell** urbanization. From here, on the rock face of the gorge, we can see the caves of the prehistoric necropolis, some of which have elaborate entrances. The cove beneath is protected by impressive cliffs.

Returning to the junction, we continue the way we were travelling to approach **La Vall d'Algaiarens**. This is a huge estate whose owners traditionally allowed families from Ciutadella to camp here in the woods close to the beautiful beach.

The luxuriant pinewoods and the marshlands have recently been catalogued as being of special interest to the environment.

For the third excursion we will leave Ciutadella from the Plaça dels Pins and head south along the Me-24, alongside the east coast. The scenery here, being a more built-up and flat area, is very different from what we have previously seen of the environs of Ciutadella. Beyond the **Cala Santandria** urbanisation we can stop at **Cala Blanca**, the best beach in the area, and then continue on to our destination at **Cap d'Artrutx**.

Before reaching the end of the road, we take the road that goes round the urbanisation to reach the lighthouse following the coastline, which here at Punta Nati, unlike in the north, is very low, with hardly any slope toward the sea, but just as rocky. On clear days, and there are few that are not, we will see the outline of Mallorca in the distance. Continuing beyond the lighthouse, we cross the urbanisations of Cala en Bosc and Son Xoriguer to the beach of the same name whose fine, white sands are characteristic of the south coast.

The best end to the trip could be a refreshing swim.

The last of the Ciutadella-based excursions must be, in turn, subdivided into three, and they all start from the Camí Vell de Sant Joan (start in Ciutadella alongside the Canal Salat).

Before leaving you should check the state of the car park in the different coves, on the panels at the entrance to the way.

(1) Firstly, we branch off at Son Vivó towards the **Son Saura** beach to visit the archaeological site at Son Catlar with its *taula*, talayots and walled precinct. It is worth making the effort to get to this beach if you intend to spend a few hours or all day there.

(2) Retracing our steps we then go on towards the **Sant Joan de Missa** Hermitage and take the Camí to Son Camaró in the direction of **Cala Turqueta**. From the car park a path takes us to the sea through a holm-oak wood that covers the ravine and adds to the charm of this lovely cove.

(3) We must return again to the hermitage with its crenulated façade and then head

Ciutadella

towards **Macarella-Macarelleta**. Along this road, which is unmade beyond the Torralba farmhouse, we will come across very few buildings as it passes through an area of large farming estates and pastures.

In 15 minutes on foot we get from the car park to the beach. The coves of Macarella and Macarelleta, both closely surrounded by dense pinewoods, are two more prime examples of the island's natural beauty. As such they have become increasingly popular with both islanders and visitors alike and, in summer, have bar facilities. The return trip provides a great view of Ciutadella and its environs.

Before closing this section, we would make one final recommendation. While travelling on the Me-1 from Ciutadella to Maó, follow the signs to the **Naveta dels Tudons** and the **Torrellafuda** settlement which are further described in the Archaeology chapter. Both routes are signposted.

4 SOUTH-EASTERN AREA

- TALATÍ DE DALT
- RAFAL RUBÍ
- SON BOU
- TORRE D'EN GAUMÉS
- TORRALBA D'EN SALORD
- SO NA CAÇANA
- CALA EN PORTER
- SANT CLIMENT
- CANUTELLS
- BINIBÈQUER
- SANT LLUÍS
- PUNTA PRIMA
- ALCALFAR
- SANT ESTEVE

Talatí de Dalt taula

Rafal Rubí naveta

On this tour we will have the opportunity to visit several archaeological sites. We take the Me-1 Maó to Alaior road and turn left just beyond the airport junction to Talatí de Dalt with its notable *taula* with lateral leaning pillar, a large, circular talayot, and several burial caves. On our way back to the main road, on a turning to the right, we can see the two navetes of **Rafal Rubí**.

At the junction just outside Alaior, we turn left on the road to **Son Bou**, the island's longest beach. The demand for tourist accommodation has resulted in the drastic reduction of the marshland area, **Es Prat**, situated behind the beach, part of which once served as rice-fields. From **Sant Jaume**, the overlooking hill, now a densely built-up area, there is a splendid view of such panoramic proportions that one can almost ignore the two monstrous, high-rise hotels that invade the horizon to our left. Apart from the usual tourist attractions, at the eastern end of the beach there is an interesting early Christian basilica and some excavated caves.

On our way back towards Alaior, we will make a detour to the right to **Torre d'en Galmés**, one of the most complete of the prehistoric settlements. Apart from the large talayots, there is much more to see, such as the enormous hypostyle chamber and the channels and water tanks that formed part of a drainage system. When the *taula* precinct was excavated, a 15cm bronze statue (circa 600 BC) of the Egyptian deity Imhotep was found, along with other items dating from prehistory through both the Roman and Moorish occupations. From here it is a short walk to the megalithic tomb at **Ses Roques Llisses**.

After returning to Alaior we will take the **Cala en Porter** road, stopping twice on the way at archaeological sites. The first, **Torralba d'en Salord**, has an enormous taula, and further on, in **So Na Caçana**, whose talayot is crowned with a geodetic measuring instrument. Shortly before the junction with the Sant Climent road. This site, has an interesting structure and notable elements. Between the two it is possible to see the curious **Torrellisar Vell** *taula*.

Cala en Porter is another spot that suffered the consequences of unplanned growth. Nevertheless, efforts have been made to rectify this as much as possible and they have managed to save the landscape of the gorge and the beauty of the estuary and deep beach. Half-way up the cliff to the left of the beach, the **Cova d'en Xoroi** is well worth a visit in the afternoons (at night there is a disco with the added attraction of spectacular moons). The cave is home to one of Menorca's most popular folk legends: that of Xoroi, an earless Moor, who on being discovered in his hideaway there, leapt to his death in the sea in order not be captured as a slave.

Cala en Porter beach

Binibèquer Vell

From Cala en Porter, we will continue via **Sant Climent** to **Cala Canutells** situated at the mouth of a gorge and important tourist centre. The entire coastline of the **Sant Lluís** area, to be visited next, is an almost continuous succession of urbanisations. They vary in age, some being more recent, but as a whole they form a long strip of white houses that wind their way along the coastline from **Binidalí** to **Punta Prima**, leaving the sparse marine vegetation behind them. Set further back from the sea, and usually on rises in the ground, we will see a number of large old mansions overlooking the coast.

At **Cala Binidalí** there is an excellent viewpoint at the top of the cliff that overlooks the cove. Along with the neighbouring **Biniparratx**, it is one of the deepest in proportion to its width, and burial caves are seen in the rocks behind both beaches.

From here on, the coastline is less rugged and flatter beyond **Cap d'en Font**. We continue along the coves of **Binisafúller**, **Binibèquer** (the largest of the three) and **Biniancolla**, all of them with beach bars and restaurants nearby. Before reaching the second one we come across the curios resort of **Binibèquer Vell**, built to imitate the traditional architectural forms of the old fishing villages. The last beach in this area, **Punta Prima**, is in the extreme south-east corner of the island. Opposite is the **Illa de l'Aire**, famous for its lighthouse and indigenous black lizards.

Cala Alcafar and **S'Algar** are also part of Sant Lluis: both are reached by turning right off the Punta Prima-Sant Lluís road. The former was the island's pioneer tourist resort, whereas S'Algar, with its hotels, villas and apartments is of more recent development and offers a wide range of facilities.

Before returning to Maó, our last stops will be **Cala Sant Esteve**, where the restored **Malborough** fort may be visited, and **Es Castell**, perhaps rounding off the day at sunset with supper at one of the restaurants in **Cales Fonts**.

Cala Mitjaneta

FROM **ES MERCADAL** TO **CALA GALDANA**

- **ES MERCADAL**
- **ES MIGJORN**
- **SANT TOMÀS**
- **SANT ADEODAT**
- **FERRERIES**
- **CALA GALDANA**

The road between Es Mercadal and Es Migjorn (Me-18) coincides with a depression between high hills that give the area a mountainous air. It starts from the old Es Mercadal barracks, converted into a trade fair and craft centre, amid tall pine trees that add to the atmosphere. Along the way we pass several old houses built on top of hillocks, probably for defensive purposes.

Es Migjorn is reached alongside the beginning of the **Binigaus gorge**, whose fertile slopes have been used for terrace farming. It is well worth visiting the town before going on to the **Sant Tomàs** and **Sant Adeodat** beaches, a tourist resort with hotels, apartments and facilities.

On the way down to these sandy areas is the turning to the prehistoric settlements of **Santa Mònica** on the left and **Sant Agustí** on the right, with a curious, hollow talayot whose roof is supported by a central pillar.

On returning to Es Migjorn, and before continuing on towards Ferreries, we can visit the talayots at **Binicodrell de Darrera**. This estate is the beginning of the old Camí de Binigaus, which starts from the cemetery. Back on the main road, it is a pleasant drive to **Ferreries** and a good view of the whole town can be seen just beyond the turning that leads to **Son Mercer**.

From Ferreries we take the Me-1 in the **Cala Galdana** direction and then, just outside the town, turn left on the Me-22 which will lead us between the **Algendar** and **Trebalúger gorges**.

We come to the turning that leads to a campsite and further on that which leads to **Cala Mitjana**, from which we can reach **Cala Trebalúger** on foot.

From the outskirts of Cala Galdana, the road drops quite steeply down to the beach which is surrounded by woodland and protected from the open sea by high cliffs. The mouth of the **Algendar gorge** serves as a canal for the mooring of small boats. Despite the presence of hotels and apartment blocks that have brought mass tourism to Cala Galdana, the natural beauty of the surroundings still place it among the most attractive of the south-coast beaches.

CYCLING ROUTES

Marked routes:

1
Ciutadella–Ferreries
17,9 kilometers, 2 hours (approx.)

2
Ferreries–Es Mercadal
14,6 kilometers, 1h 45m (approx.)

3
Es Mercadal–Alaior
7,3 kilometers, 45 minutes (approx.)

4
Alaior–Maó
12,2 kilometers, 1h 15m (approx.)

5
Maó–Es Castell
8,4 kilometers, 45 minutes (approx.)

6
Es Castell–Sant Lluís
6,3 kilometers, 35 minutes (approx.)

7
Sant Lluís–Punta Prima
5,3 kilometers, 30 minutes (approx.)

All have the qualification of low difficulty, that supposes his use by beginners, except the 2nd, considered of medium difficulty.

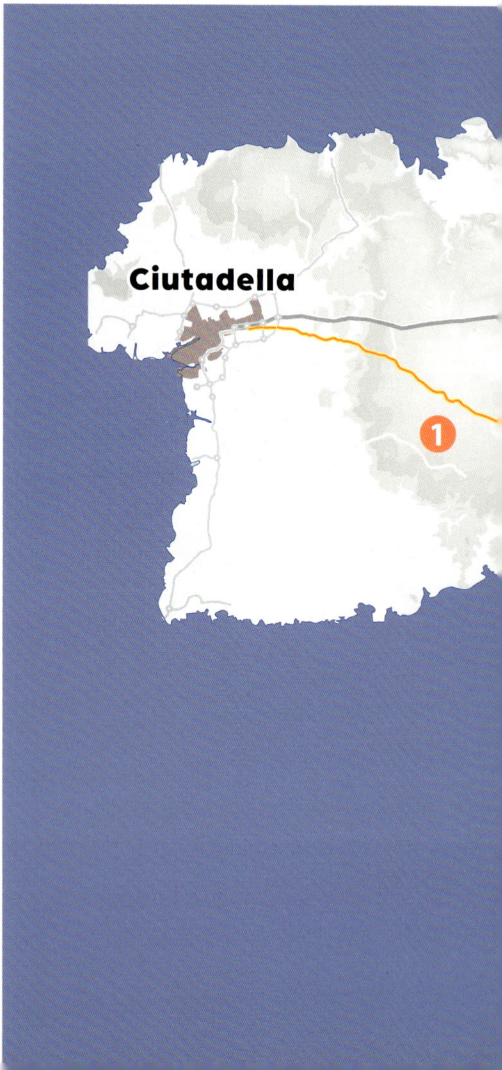

Fornells
2
Ferreries
es Mercadal
3
Alaior
es Migjorn Gran
4
Maó
es Castell
5
Sant Lluís
6
7
Punta Prima

INFORMATION AND SUGGESTIONS

This section provides you with further information regarding what we have already described so that you will be able to make the very most of the island and its customs. It is not, however, exhaustive in terms of the practical addresses, which often change and this information can always be obtained from the local official sources.

ART AND CULTURE

Menorca has always been attractive for those seeking out muses. Artists, both local and from afar, have tried over the centuries to express the island's beauty and mystery in their works of art.

PAINTING

Painting has always been a particularly fruitful field with a marked emphasis on landscape painting in which the island's special quality of light has always played an important role. In the 18th century, the Italian **Giuseppe Chiesa** (1720-1789), who set up residence here following his marriage to a Menorcan woman, left an important pictorial record of the island at that time and introduced the Italian naturalist influence known as *veduta*. His Menorcan disciple **Pascual Calbó** (1752-1817) was famous for both his scientific treatises and his artistic qualities.

In the nineteenth century, the wide seascapes of Maó harbour under stormy skies, painted by **Font** (1811-1885), were recurrent examples of the romantic school of the time. **Hernández Monjo** (1862-1937) also left a legacy of seascapes, full of light and colour, in this case in the turn of the century realist-modernist style.

Contemporary art is represented by two important landscape painters: **Joan Vives Llull** (1901-1982) in whose impressionist work nature is the most important element, and **Josep Torrent** (1904-1990), Ciutadella-born expressionist, whose original technique captures the essence and rhythm of the island. Also from Ciutadella, **Maties Quetglas** (1946), who has lived and worked in Madrid for some years, is known both nationally and internationally among the hyper-realist school.

Continuing its historical tradition, Menorca enjoys an artistic activity and great richness and variety of techniques.

Also thanks to its rich history, architecture has an important place in Menorca. Whether military fortifications of great interest and size or buildings and palaces of diverse and interesting architectural styles.

To discover all this cultural richness, both artistic and architectural, we suggest a selection of places that you can visit in different districts:

MUSEUMS AND ART GALLERIES

Maó

Fortress of La Mola. Guided tours daily. One of the major European fortifications of the 19th century built between 1848 and1875 by order of Isabel II. Today it has lost its military use and has a cultural and tourist role. Guided visits during the day and at night, exhibitions and other activities. T 971 364 040 www.fortalesalamola.com

Museum of Menorca. In the old convent of Sant Francesc. Both the setting and the contents are of great interest. Unique items from all periods illustrate the changes and socio-cultural evolution of Menorca from prehistoric times to today. Avda/ Dr. Guàrdia. T 971 350 955 www.museudemenorca.com

Ca n'Oliver. Museum project in a splendid stately palace from the early 19th century in neoclassical style which features a stairway with a fresco by Giuseppe Patania. It houses a selection of engravings from the art collection of the Consell Insular de Menorca (local authority) and pieces from the collection of the former Hernández Sanz-Hernández Mora Museum. It also has temporary exhibition rooms. Anuncivay, 2.
T 971 350 597

Sala de Cultura "La Caixa". Multidisciplinary room in which different activities are organised. Nou, 25.

Sala de Cultura "Sa Nostra". Situated in the old St. Antoni church, S'Arraval 32, holds temporary exhibitions all year round. S'Arraval, 32. T 971 366 854

Claustre del Carme. Temporary exhibitions. Plaça Miranda.

The Scientific, Literary and Artistic Athenaeum. Works by *Vives Llull*, collections of drawings and paintings, Menorcan natural history exhibition. Cultural and sociological lectures are given all year round.
Sa Rovellada de Dalt, 25.
T 971 360 553
www.ateneumao.org

Galeria Artara. Temporary and permanent exhibitions.
Rosari, 18. T 971 352 912
www.galeriaartara.com

Galeria d'Art Kroma. Temporary and permanent exhibitions.
Anuncivay, 7. T 971 350 804

Galeria Encant. Temporary and permanent exhibitions.
Infanta, 20. T 971 364 416
www.encant.net

Ciutadella

Ciutadella City Museum "Bastió de sa Font". History, archaeology and ethnology. Plaça de sa Font.
T 971 380 297
www.ajciutadella.org

Municipal Hall in the Roser church. On the street of the same name. Temporary exhibitions throughout the year.
T 971 383 563

Diocesan Museum. Adjoined to the Seminary, it contains very rare and old exhibits of historical and religious value. It also houses the Pere Daura collection of contemporary painting. Seminari, 7.
T 971 481 297

Galería Vidrart. Temporary and permanent exhibitions.
Roser, 8. T 971 385 851
www.galeriavidrart.com

Galeria Retxa. Temporary and permanent exhibitions
Nou de Juliol, 37. T 971 381 806
www.galeriaretxa.com

Pedreres de s´Hostal. Spectacular series of old and modern quarries, run by Líthica, an association that safeguards it and organises cultural activities of theatre, concerts and artistic representations in the space. Two km. from Ciutadella on the Camí Vell de Maó.
T 971 481 578, www.lithica.es

Sant Joan de Missa (hermitage). Open Mondays from 4 to 7 p.m.

Alaior

Centre Internacional d'Art i Gravat de Menorca. Located in the Antiga Escola des Ramal, a building of unusual architecture, is this workshop-school of graphic arts in which exhibitions and cultural activities are also organised.
Baixamar, 54-56 .
www.gravatmenorca.org

Sala Municipal d'Art. Temporary exhibitions. Major, 11.

Sant Diego Cultural Centre. In the old church of the same name. Temporary exhibitions.

Es Castell

Fort Malborough, Spectacular fort of British origin built between 1710 and 1726, and can be visited inside. Cala Sant Esteve.
T 971 360 462

Sant Felip Castle . Visits by arrangement, the night-time ones being of particular interest. Road to Cala Sant Esteve. T 971 361 000

Military Museum of Menorca. Plaça Esplanada. T 971 362 100.
www.museomilitarmenorca.com

Es Mercadal

Centre Artesanal de Menorca. An opportunity to see together the work of the majority of the island's craftpeople and buy their pieces.
T 971 154 436
www.artesaniademenorca.com

Torre de Fornells. Defensive tower built by the English between 1801 and 1802. It can be visited in summer only, Mondays to Fridays, from 9:30 to 15h, Saturdays and Sundays from 10 to 14:45 h.

Pasearte Fornells. A self-run space where you can buy all types of arts and crafts. It organises exhibitions and live concerts. From June to September, every day in the afternoon and evening. Rosari.

Es Migjorn Gran

Galerias Es Migjorn Gran, watercolours by Graham Byfield. Open from April to October.
Sant Llorenç, 12-1

Migjornale. Festival of art that turns streets, public spaces and private homes into exhibition "rooms". It is organised biennially for two days in August.

Ferreries

Museu Rural i de les Ciències Naturals de Menorca, Binissuès. Tradition and history are combined in a unique spot, a visit that will allow you to relive life in rural Menorca. It also has a collection of 8,000 insects of the Carreras Torrent brothers. Ctra. Maó-Ciutadella, km 31.6, at the turning of the Camí dels Alocs. T 971 380 056

Fosquets d'Art. Art also invades the town of Ferreries. An artistic initiative organised by the Art's association which it undertakes every two years at the beginning of August.

Sant Lluís

Es Molí de Dalt. Ethnological museum with a large selection of work tools, installed in a flour mill restored to the minutest detail.
Es Cós, 4. T 971 151 084

MUSIC

The visitor may be surprised by the variety of musical activities that take place on the island and, indeed, by the very high standard of the performances. Menorcans are, by tradition, a music-loving people.

OPERA AND CLASSICAL MUSIC

The **Asociación Amics de s'Òpera** and the **Fundació Menorquina de la Òpera** prepare a lyrical season every year with the performance of an opera, usually between the end of May and the beginning of June. They also organise different activities to bring opera closer to a broad public.
Another very active group is **Joventuts Musicals**. From October to May they give concerts, usually weekly, by leading musicians. During July and August they hold **Summer Music Festivals** which take place in Ciutadella and Maó, where the OCIM, **Orquestra de Câmara de l'Illa de Menorca**, is the resident orchestra, as well the **Nits de Música Clàssica** that are held in the parish church of Fornells during August.

In July and August an "International Concert Cycle" is organised by the **Sta. María Organ Foundation** with top soloists in this instrument. You can also attend the *"Matins a l'Orgue"*, morning sessions lasting half an hour in the summer, and the weekly afternoon concert.

In the cloister of the Convent of Socors in Ciutadella, both singing and organ auditions are held throughout the year by the **Capella Davídica**. Here the voice of the world-famous, Ciutadella-born baritone *Joan Pons*, pride of the island, and currently considered among the world's finest, was trained. Among other activities, they organise the *"Balearic Islands International Organ Week"* in the cathedral in February or March, and Easter, summer and Christmas concerts, which also feature performances in different towns.

JAZZ

Although not such a long-standing tradition among the Menorcans, jazz does have a place in the island's musical scene.
Highly recommended are the sessions organised by *Jazz Obert, Associació d'Al·ligàtors:* especially its Festival **MENORCA JAZZ** in spring, but also other concerts throughout the year; see programme at www.jazzobert.com. Another interesting offer is that of the jam sessions in the Casino de Sant Climent, from Easter until the end of October

FOLK

The folk groups are also experiencing a boom and are increasingly performing at events organised outside the island.

The *Menorcan Jota*, sung and danced, are ever-present in the local festivals and there are always concerts of *habaneras,* shanty songs, that remind the people of Menorca of the times when they emigrated to Cuba as well as recitals of *glosat*, verse.

LIVE MUSIC

Jazz, rock and folk concerts are held throughout the year in Maó, Ciutadella and other points of the island with the participation of both local and visiting musicians.
Maó is famous for the programming of what is called **Música al Carrer** and **Nits al Port**, when during the summer on Tuesdays and Thursdays musicians take to the street.
Also in summer in **Sa Terrassa des Claustre** there are a large variety of live concerts organised. In Maó harbour, the bar **Akelarre**, on Moll de Ponent has live jazz and rock throughout the year. In Ciutadella, for live music go to the **Jazzbah** bar, in Pla de Sant Joan.

THEATRE

The emblematic **Teatre Principal**, run by a Foundation, is one of the main centres that hosts the increasingly frequent theatrical performances in (www.teatremao.com).
The **Cercle Artístic**, a prestigious cultural society in Ciutadella (www.cercleartistic.com) awards the *Es Born de Teatre Prize* each year, an award with growing importance within the Catalan theatre scene.
Also of note are the *"Aules de Teatre"*, theatre workshops that are dedicated to giving actors more training, fantastically successful in its aims.

Of recent construction stands the Albert Camús multifunctional hall in Sant Lluís, a multidisciplinary artistic centre which features plays, dance or audio-visual screenings, among other activities.

The love of different disciplines of the stage arts goes back a long way, however, as can be seen by the presence of small theatre spaces in different towns that have been used from the late-19th century until today. Here, amateur groups provide their neighbours with stage productions that do not lack ambition, and the mass attendance at these shows ensures their survival. In Ciutadella, for example, it is traditional for, coinciding with the Sant Joan Festivals, a performance of *Foc i Fum* to be given, a work written by the Ciutadela-born **Joan Benejam i Vives** in 1885. Also regularly performed is *"El viatge tràgic de l'amo en Xec de s'Uestrà"*, written in the early 20th century by **Ángel Ruíz i Pablo**, from Es Castell.

As well as the longstanding associations, such as the **Orfeó Maonés** or the **Delfí Serra**, **Sant Miquel** and **Mô Teatre** groups, other, newer, groups have been formed such as **La Clota** and **Teatre de Xoc**, with their own productions.

LITERATURE

Menorca's contribution to Catalan and European culture has been quite considerable, although it remains comparatively unknown to the public in general. After the foundation in 1778 of the Societat Maonesa de Cultura, there was intense activity in this field within the enlightened trends of the times. Many members of this group studied in the south of France, such as **Joan Ramis i Ramis**, the leading exponent of Catalan neoclassic drama whose works include *Lucrècia* (1769), in defence of republican liberties, and *Arminda i Rosaura o el més constant amor*. At this time, works by Molière, Goldoni, Metastasio etc., were translated on the island and linguistic treatises published, such as the *Principis de lectura menorquina*, in which the author **Febrer i Cardona** clearly defined the unity of the vernacular language within Catalan territories.

Scientific literature was particularly represented by the work of **Dr. Orfila i Rotger** (1787-1853) who studied chemistry and medicine in Paris and whose studies on toxicology enjoyed great prestige. He was physician to Louis XVIII of France and chair of chemistry at the University of Paris.

These predecessors undoubtedly sowed the seeds for all the literature that has been published in the Menorca of today, *Folklore menorquí de la pagesia* by **Francesc d'Albranca** being one of the best-known works, as well as the recent narrative work by the award-winning **Pau Faner**. Nor should we ignore the poetic work of **Gumersind Riera**, **Pere Gomila** or **Ponç Pons**. A full list of authors would be too long for this space, so we recommend readers to head for the specialist bookshops, where all the aforementioned works can be found.

We should also mention the *Revista de Menorca*, published since 1888 by the **Scientific, Literary and Artistic Athenaeum of Maò**, as well as the *Enciclopèdia de Menorca,* created by the now-disappeared **Obra Cultural Balear**, and now run by the **Fundació Enciclopèdia de Menorca** which studies all aspects of Menorca reality. It accepts subscribers.

Contemporary fiction and poetry is also represented on the island, and a local author, Pau Faner, has won national literary awards. All the aforementioned works can be found in the island's book-shops along with any new publications by native writers.

RECOMMENDED READING

English editions

- Ferri, M. José. **Menorca, Biosphere Reserve**. Triangle Postals, 2016.
- Lara, Sergi. **The Camí de Cavalls, the tour of Menorca**. Triangle Postals , 2012.
- Sintes, Elena. **Talayotic Minorca, the island's prehistory**. Triangle Postals , 2015.
- Villier, Marcel. **Architecture and landscape of Menorca**. Triangle Postals , 2015.
- V.V.AA. **Portum, Stories of Minorca**. Empatic, 2016.

Editions in Catalan and Spanish

- Armstrong, John. **Historia de la isla de Menorca**. Edit. Nura, 1978.
- Arxiu Sturla. **Menorca, record d'un temps**. Triangle Postals, 2005.
- Ballester, Pedro. **De re cibaria**. (Menorcan cuisine and cakemaking) Edit. Puig, 1995.
- Borràs, Josep, y Borràs, Damià. **La cocina de Menorca**. Viena, 2014.
- Camps, Esperança. **La draga**. Llibres del delicte, 2017.
- Camps i Mercadal, F. (Francesc d'Albranca). **Folklore Menorquí**, 1987.
- Casasnovas Camps, Miquel Àngel. **Història de Menorca**. Editorial Moll, 2015.
- Casasnovas Marquès, Andreu. **El patrimoni artístic de Menorca**. Ed. Nura, 2003.
- Castells, Ada. **Pura Sang**. Edicions 62, 2012.
- Cultura Popular, **Quaderns de Folklore**. Ciutadella.
- Escandell Salom, Antoni. **Peixos de Menorca**. 1998.

• Faner, Pau. **L'amor del capità Gavina**. Meteora, 2016.

• Florit, F. i Sauleau, L. **Pedreres de Marès**. Líthica, 1995.

• Garrido, Carlos. **Menorca mágica**. Olañeta, 1990.

• Marfany, Marta. **Els menorquins d'Algèria**. Pròleg de Joan Pons. I.M.E., 2002.

• Nooteboom, Cees. **Lluvia Roja**. Siruela, 2012.

• Pons, Ponç. **El rastre blau de les formigues**. Editorial Arrela, 2014.

• Pons, Ponç. **Memorial de Tabarka**. Cruïlla, 1993.

• Quintana, Josep Maria. **Los Nikolaidis**. Editorial Milenio, 2017.

• Ramón-Cortés, Ferran. **L'illa dels cinc fars. Les claus de la comunicació**. Portic, 2012.

• Rosell i Sanuy, Joan, i Llompart i Díaz, Carme. **El naixement d'una illa : Menorca : guia de geologia pràctica**. : IME, 2002.

• Sabrafin, Gabriel. **Cuentos fabulosos y leyendas de las islas**. Olañeta, 1988.

• Salord, Maite. **L'alè de les cendres**. Editorial Arrela, 2014.

• Vidal, Toni. **Menorca, tot just ahir**. Triangle Postals, 2000.

• Vidal, Toni. **Roques de Menorca**. Triangle Postals, 2005.

• Vuillier, Gaston. **Les Illes Oblidades**. Edit. Moll, 1973.

• V.V.AA. Quaderns Xibau. **Col·lecció de Poesia Contemporània**. I.M.E., 1990/95.

HANDICRAFTS

Today the most outstanding traditional arts and crafts are confined on the island to pottery and the manufacture of *avarques* sandals, typical peasant sandals. However, basket-making, costume jewellery, leather work, textile and paper serigraphy are still carried out.

The **Centre Artesanal de Menorca**, situated in Mercadal, was created with the idea of promoting and recovering Menorcan arts and crafts. It has a permanent exhibition of craft trades and information about all the arts and crafts activity on the island

Traditional Menorcan pottery is characterized by its use of local raw materials and the distinctive forms of the finished articles. They are kiln-baked pieces, unglazed, and often not even polished. They have a special charm, the most curious pieces being jugs (*barca, cul estret, castanyes*), bottles (*buldrofa, ses botilles*), clay pipes with wooden mouthpieces, pitchers (the bucket used in wells), earthenware bowls, *maridets* (for warming up the sheets), drinking and feeding troughs for farm animals, urns for plants...

You can find traditional ceramics in a large variety of shops on the island, above all in the ports and commercial areas of Maó and Ciutadella as well as in the markets in all the districts.

Also in the eastern area, four craftsmen offer a ceramic route where you can watch the pieces being made in their own style, visiting the workshops situated in rural areas with a special charm; arrange visits by calling:

Es Fangueti, T 971 369 598
A. Vico, T 971 369 128
Remi Lora, T 606 248 036
Magda Cardona, T 629 490 366

As in this field, in which there are many more shops that sell typical or contemporary ceramics, there are also many shops where you can find *avarques*, but if you want direct contact with the craftsmen you should go to **Can Doblas Artesania** in Plaça Jaume II, in Ferreries. www.candoblas.com

On the other hand, high-quality footwear (and other leather goods) can be bought in the shops of the selfsame manufacturers, where in theory the prices are lower than in the normal retail outlets. There are many of these on the industrial estates, particularly in Ciutadella and Ferreries, and you can also order made-to-measure shoes in some small factories.

Other examples of local handicrafts can be found at the outdoor markets which take place daily in the summer and weekly the rest of the year: **Ses Voltes** and **S'Esplanada** (Maó), **Baixada Camplionch** (Ciutadella harbour), **Baixada Cales Fonts** (Es Castell) and the handicraft markets of Mercadal and Alaior. On Saturday mornings an interesting market is held in Ferreries where local farmers sell products such as honey, cheese, jam and preserves.

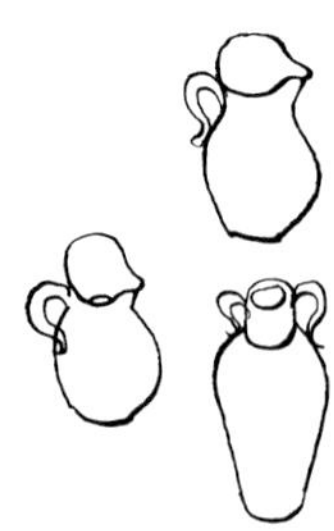

ANTIQUES

The fact that antique dealers are to be found in most of the towns is hardly surprising on an island that has been enriched throughout its history by contributions from many different cultures. From the ancient civilizations, the remains of the Talayotic era that form part of Menorca's unique and protected archaeological heritage are the first examples, and are followed by Phoenician amphorae retrieved from the sea bed and Roman objects that have been discovered in the course of excavation and building work. Not to be forgotten are the fossils, nature's own "antiques", brought to light after millennia by the erosion of the elements.

The British and French dominations left in their wake an important legacy of characteristic everyday objects which, in the course of time, have become sought-after antiques. A prime example is the 18th century Chippendale and Sheraton furniture imported, in the main, during the last British occupation. The furniture found its way, over the years, through inheritance or sale, into homes of all social levels. Occasionally, authentic pieces can still be found for sale. Even locally-made rustic furniture came under the English influence and is more refined and sophisticated than its counterparts elsewhere.

Many other decorative objects, paintings, trinkets and valuables of varied origins, dating principally from the 17th to 20th centuries.

Due to the fact that quality items are intermixed with the simpler pieces and that the prices vary according to their category and the restoration work involved, we will not give you any addresses or more precise advice. Antique-lovers will know where to find them, mainly in Maó and Ciutadella, and we are not going to spoil the added fun that finding the best objects by your own means involves.

FESTIVALS

The horse is the undisputed symbol of the Festivals of Menorca and we have already mentioned those of Ciutadella and Maó. They are held in honour of the patron saint of the town and give rise to sporting and cultural activities as well as religious celebrations. The first note of the ***tambor*** and ***flabiol*** (the drum and the pipe) is the anxiously awaited sound that signals the start of the ***colcada*** or procession. With the exception of Ciutadella, where centuries-old rituals surround and determine the course of the festivities which reach their climax with the ***Jocs des Pla*** tournament, the *colcada* and *jaleo* take place on the afternoon of the saint's day and the following morning. In recent years, the old tradition of the ***Corregudes des Cós***, or horse racing in the street, has been revived in Maó and the townspeople take part enthusiastically.

Festivities in honour of the patron saints are not the only fêtes that are celebrated. As befits a Mediterranean culture, Menorcans maintain many Christian and pagan traditions, and there are quite a few of them throughout the year.

CALENDAR OF FESTIVALS

January

St. Anthony's Day (patron saint of Menorca) in commemoration of the conquest of the island by Alfons III: **16th**, street parties with bonfires and toast and *sobrasada* called *torrades*.

17th Activities in all the towns. In Ciutadella a traditional market is held in Pl. de l'Hospital and a procession of the *Tres Tocs*.

February, March, April.

Carnival. Variable, depending on the religious calendar. Fancy dress balls and processions of floats in all the towns. Particularly original are the Black and White Ball in Es Migjorn and the *Ball de ses Tauletes* at the Casino Nou in Ciutadella, both on the Monday.

Easter. Variable. Processions and religious ceremonies all over the island. Of particular interest are: on **Good Friday**, the Procession of the Holy Burial in Maó and the procession in Es Migjorn of very ancient origin. On **Easter Saturday** they hold the Sacred Concert at Ciutadella Cathedral with religious ceremonies that conclude with the *Foc Nou* in the cathedral square.

Easter Sunday sees the procession of the *Encontre* in Maó and Es Migjorn. In Ciutadella at noon, a bonfire set alight by shots from a blunderbuss. In many towns there is choir singing in the streets, the traditional *deixem lo dol.*

Whitsun. Variable. Traditional outings and picnics in the country and beaches from Ciutadella and Ferreries.

May

Ses Coques de Sant Josep. **1st** Sunday in Ferreries, cakes and pastries are blessed and sold in benefit of the parish.

15th St. Isidore's Day. Patron saint of farmers. Religious and sporting events at the Hermitage of Fàtima

24th or the following Sunday. **Procession of Maria Auxiliadora** in Ciutadella. Religious ceremony and procession through the old part of the city. At Sa Contramurada, a concert by the Municipal Band and a street dance.

June

Dia des Be. On the Sunday prior to St. John's Day, a beautiful sheep, adorned with coloured ribbons is carried through the streets in a clear homage to Bautista, accompanied by a piper to announce the beginning of the festivities.

23rd-24th: after vespers at the church of St. Joan de Missa, the city goes crazy in celebrating its main festival: hazelnut battles, *jaleo*, *colcades*, *caragols*..., until it is the turn of the equestrian games which take place in Es Pla: *ses carotes, ses ensortilles, córrer abraçats*...

29th St. Peter's Day (or the following weekend). Seafarer's festival in the Port of Maó. With typical games, such as *es capellet*, shanty song recitals and open-air dances. There are also classical sailing and rowing regattas.

July

9th: Commemoration of the Turkish assault on Ciutadella in 1558, the year of the tragedy (*S'any de sa desgràcia*). **The Act of Constantinople** is read in public and the *Junta de Caixers* is chosen for the next year.

10th: St. Christopher's Day festivities where vehicles are blessed and there is folk dancing and open-air dances.

Sea processions of Carmen.
15th-16th: The image of the Virgin of Carmen is carried around the harbours of Maó, Ciutadella and Fornells by a procession of boats of all kinds that are decorated with lights and garlands of flowers and images of the Virgin of Carmen.

24th-25th: St. James's Day festivals in Es Castell.

3rd weekend: St. Martin's Day festivals in Mercadal.

4th weekend: St. Anthony's Day festivities in Fornells.

5th weekend (or first in August): **St. Christopher's Day** festivities in Es Migjorn.

August

1st weekend: St. Gaietà's Day festivals in Llucmassanes.

1st weekend after the 10th: **St. Lawrence's Day** festivals in Alaior.

3rd weekend: **St. Clement's Day** festivals in St. Climent .

23rd-25th: St. Bartholomew's Day festivals in Ferreries.

Last weekend: St. Louis's Day festivals in St. Lluís

September

7th-8th: Our Lady of Grace festivals in Maó. Wide range of celebratory acts, featuring the ancient and revived *Corregudes des Cós* horse races.

29th: St. Michael's Day festivities in Es Migjorn with horses and *jaleo* every fifth year.

November

1st: All Saints' Day. Traditional doughnuts with honey are sold all over the island.

December

25th: The traditional nativity play, "Els Pastorells" is performed in several towns. Exhibitions of nativity scenes in Maó and in Ciutadella, a tour of the different nativity scenes prepared at different parts of the city, featuring those at the Seminary and Santa Clara church.

31st: The New Year is celebrated at midnight by the ringing of bells in town squares and at public dances.

OTHER FOLK TRADITIONS

Codolades

These are popular poetic compositions, usually of a satiric nature, whose metre differs in Menorca from other places. They tend to make reference to local or collective situations and affairs.

Glosats

Poetic compositions improvised by different people in turn, who exchange cutting remarks, fitting it into a very strict strophic and syllabic pattern, accompanied by the guitar that marks the rhythm. Both these examples of traditional folk culture have been kept alive thanks to several groups who periodically give performances all over the island.

SPORT

Over recent years the offer for sports fan has increased with the creation of new sports facilities, as well the organisation of competitions and exhibition and practice sessions. Access to the first division of the ACB of the Menorca Básquet team from 2005 to 2012 meant the construction on the island of a multifunctional sports centre with a capacity for over five thousand people. In fact, nearly all the towns have their own sports centre and there are also facilities in many hotels and urbanisations.

Apart from competitive sports, such as football or basketball, the tournaments in which only federation-registered teams can play, and the sports schools of excellence that the different councils possess, here we will only mention the facilities or sports that are open to the occasional visitor.

Cricket

The large number of British residents on the island has given rise to the formation of a cricket club, the **Menorca Cricket Club** (or M.C.C.) to be found on the Biniparrell road, near St. Lluís, has the only grass cricket pitch in Spain, as well as the usual facilities. Competitive matches are usually played on a Saturday, sometimes between foreign and local teams.
www.menorcacricketclub.com

Golf

Excellent facilities (eighteen holes) are to be found in the only golf course on the island, the **Club Son Parc**, situated in the urbanisation of the same name in Es Mercadal.
T 971 188 875
www.clubsonparc.com

Horse sports

We have already mentioned the important role the horse has always played in the festivals on the island, but the love of horses and the care of them goes well beyond that. There are competitions each year to preserve the appearance and qualities of the indigenous race of black horses and there are many possibilities for equestrian activities, the main ones being listed below.

At the hippodromes in Maó (Carretera de Maó a Sant Lluís, T 606 346 901, www.hipodrommunicipaldemao.cat) and Ciutadella (Torre del Ram, T 971 388 038), on the majority of Sundays and bank holidays there are attractive trotting and galloping races, along with the usual betting. In summer, the **Ganadería son Martorellet** de Ferreries (Cala Galdana road), performs an equestrian show on Tuesdays and Thursdays from 8.30 p.m. onwards. (T 971 373 406, www.sonmartorellet.com). In the clubs linked to the island branch of the **Balearic Equestrian Federation** (T 971 154 225), they give classes in Menorcan and classical taming, and there are also horses for learning to ride or for horse-riding trips.

There are many centres that offer tourists horse-riding trips, the main ones being:

Son Bou Rutas a Caballo.
Torre Solí Nou, Atalis (parking)
T 619 841 521,
www.sonbourutasacaballo.com

Cavalls Son Àngel.
Camí d'Algaiarens.
T 609 833 902
www.cavallssonangel.com

Menorca Equus.
Camí del Pilar
T 609 239 850 | 638 845 774
www.menorcaequus.com

Petit Russó.
Camí de Macarella
(Finca Bellaventura)
T 696 964 058 | 639 993 160
www.petitrusso.com

Rutas Ecuestres Camí de Cavalls. Algaiarens, 14.
T 636 455 270 | 620 102 219.
www.rutasecuestrescamicavalls.com

Yeguada San Adeodato.
Platja de Sant Adeodat
T 667 073 385
www.yeguadasanadeodato.es

"Ferradura" Horse Riding Centre.
Centro Ecuestre Equimar, Camí Verd. Tel. 669 255 487
www.menorcahorseriding.com

Menorca a Cavall.
Crta. Cala Galdana, km 4,3
Finca es Calafat.
T 971 374 637 | 626 593 737
www.menorcaacavall.com

Tennis

The growing popularity for this sport has led to a proliferation of municipal tennis courts in the towns and also in some hotels and urbanisations. Among other clubs, we can mention here:
C.T. Maó, T 971 365 703;
C.T. Malbuger, T 971 362 535;
C.T. S'Algar, T 971 150 361;
C.T. Ciutadella, T 971 388 456;
C.T. Oar, T 971 482 631;
C.T. Alaior, T 971 378 618;
C.T. Mercadal, T971 375 523

In many of these installations there are also paddle courts.

OTHER ALTERNATIVES

At the flying club **Aeroclub Menorca** (road Maó-Sant Lluís, T 971 361 672; www.aeroclubmenorca.com), light aircraft flights can be arranged and offer the chance to discover the island from the air. They also have a go-kart circuit.

The **GOB** (Balearic ornithology Group) also offers an alternative way of discovering the island. It organises excursions for small groups, with routes around the countryside, the beach or archaeological routes. There are also interesting activities for ornithologists and all nature lovers. In Maó, Camí des Castell, 53, from 9 a.m. to 3 p.m. T 35 07 62 and www.gobmenorca.com.

Traditional sports. Of the games that entertained people in the past, only reminiscences remain. One of them, however, a game called ***La Bolla***, is still played in just one place in Sant Lluís, inside the bar La Bolla, Es Cós, no. 56. Its similarity in some aspects to petanque indicates it has been played since the time of the French occupation.

Another game, ***Joc Maonés***, also unique, is more like martial arts than a game. Reserved until now to just a few fans and masters who know the rules handed down by word of mouth generation to generation. It is renowned for the singular elegance of the steps, *tocs* which increase in intensity prior to the combat itself, *rodar*.

WATER SPORTS

As far as these activities are concerned, the possibilities seem endless. From sailing boats to pedalos, windsurf boards and motorboats, almost every kind of craft is available for hire. Also it has grown the use of the kayak, that allow to stroll along the coast discovering remote places of big beauty. During the year occur meetings of local practitioners but is in the summer when increases its practical with the improvement of the environmental conditions. Two addresses to take into account for rent crafts of this type are: **Menorca en kayak**, Es Grau (T 669 097 977, www.menorcaenkayak.com) and **Dia complert**, Fornells (T 609 670 996, www.diacomplert.com).

Excellent nautical sports facilities and services exist in Maó, Ciutadella and Fornells and, also, in many holiday centres. Visitors should bear in mind, however, that in the high season the demand for craft for hire is far greater than the supply. Below is a brief guide of where you can go to pursue nautical sports on the island.

In the Port of Maó they hire sailing and motor boats at **Nautic Fun** (T 971 364 250, www.nauticfunmenorca.com) in Sa Colàrsega, and also at **Menorca Nàutic** (T 971 354 543, www.menorcanautic.com) in the Moll de Llevant. But if you prefer a simple sail around the inside of the port, you should go to Moll de Ponent and climb aboard any of the craft that leave from there for trips that last around one hour, with commentaries in different languages and the majority of boats with a glass bottom in order to be able to see the underwater scenery. We would highlight from among these boats the **Yellow Catamarans**, T 639 676 351, www. ellowcatamarans.com.

In the Port de Fornells, which we have already mentioned that is a perfect spot for water sports, you can also hire motor or rowing boats at **Servi-Nàutic Menorca**, T 629 273 209 www.servinauticmenorca.com, and surfboards, sailing boats and catamarans at **Wind Fornells**, T 664 335 801, www.windfornells.com. The **Club Náutico de Fornells** is an important sailing school. T 971 376 328 www.cnfornells.com

From the port of Ciutadella and from Cala Galdana boats leave for the beaches on the south coast. Some of them also have a glass bottom, making the routes they take more interesting. You can also hire boats in the port of Ciutadella at, for example, **Menorcaboats**, Moll Comercial Marina, 66, Moll Comercial, T 971 484 281, www.menorcaboats.com

For more information, contact: **the Balearic Sailing Federation**
T 971 402 412
www.federacionbalearvela.org

DIVING

In the diving centres you can go diving with all the material and help necessary.

Blue Dive Menorca
Zona Comercial, 7-8, Port d'Addaia.
T 971 940 251
www.bluedivemenorca.com

Son Bou Scuba
Centre Comercial Sant Jaume, s/n
Son Bou. T 696 628 26
www.sonbouscuba.com

Bluewater Scuba
Cala en Bosc. T 971 387 183
www.bluewaterscuba.co.uk

Centro de Buceo Poseidón
Cala Santandria. T 971 382 644
www.bahia-poseidon.de

Club Nàutic de Ciutadella
Camí de Baix, s/n. T 971 383 918
www.cnciutadella.com

Dive Inn Menorca
Pla de Sant Joan, 10.
T 651 644 319 | 608 864 007
www.diveinnmenorca.com

Happy Sub Diving Center
Hotel Almirante Farragut,
Cala en Forcat. T 609 213 329
www.happysub.de

Scuba Plus
Cala en Busquets, 10.
T 696 903 160
www.scubaplus.org

Diving Center Fornells
Passeig Maritim, 68
T 971 376 431
www.divingfornells.com

Diving Menorca
Hotel Club Carema Playa Playas de Fornells. T 625 712 631
www.divingmenorca.com

ACCOMMODATION

The supply of big hotels, guest houses and apartments is well known, so we will not give a massive list of places. We will only give you an idea of some places of an alternative nature which contribute to preserving the environment. They are small hotels that respect the relationship between the landscape and the typical architecture without ignoring the quality of service and comfort. What usually happens is that, by having such a small space available, it is almost essential to book in advance. Her we offer a few examples:

Hotel del Almirante. Colonial-type construction –very well remodelled– from the 18th century. Admiral Collingwood, a contemporary of Nelson, lived in it. A beautiful garden, swimming pool and tennis courts, it is famous for having a haunted room. On the road between Maó and Es Castell, T 971 362 700
www. hoteldelalmirante.com

S'Engolidor. An old country house now absorbed into the town. Hostel-restaurant with just five rooms. Good facilities, respecting the original decoration, and famous for its typical Menorcan cuisine. Pleasant garden overlooking the ravine. It is in Es Migjorn Gran, Major, 3.
T 971 370 193, www.sengolidor.com

Menorca Hotel Association. Information and telephone bookings
T 971 361 003, www.visitmenorca.com

AGROTOURISM

Other options are what are called rural tourism and agrotourism, based in country houses, places which have been adapted to accommodate all those who love the rural life and nature.
www.menorcaturismorural.net

Alaior

Turmaden des Capità.
Ctra. de Es Migjorn, Km 1.
T 971 37 80 65
www.turmaden.com

Santa Mariana.
Crta. Maó - Ciutadella, km 9,5
T 622 513 364
www.santamarianamenorca.com

Torralbenc.
Ctra. Maó-Cala en Porter, km 10
T 971 377 211, www.torralbenc.com

Ciutadella

Sant Tomàs de Vilanova.
Camí Vell, km 3. T 646 278 537

Biniatram. Crta. Cala Morell, after the junction with the Algaiarens path. T 971 383 113
www.biniatram.com

Ferreries

Son Triay Nou. Crta. Cala Galdana, km 2,3.
T 971 155 078 | 600 074 441
www.sontriay.com

Ca na Xini. Camí de Sant Patrici.
T 971 374 512, www.canaxini.com

Binisaid. Crta. Cala Galdana, km 4,3. T 971 155 063 | 971 352 303
www.binisaid.com

Son Triay.
Crta. Cala Galdana, km 2,5
T 971 155 078, www.sontriay.com

Finca Atalis. Es Migjorn Gran.
At the end of Sant Tomàs urbanization. T 971 370 461 | 678 454 123
www.fincaatalis.com

Maó

Llucmaçanes Gran. In the town of Llucmaçanes, close to Maó. Pla de Sant Gaietà, 10.
T 971 352 117, www.llucmagran.com

Matxaní Gran. Sant Climent.
Crta. de Sant Climent a Binidalí.
T 971 153 337
www.menorcacountryhouse.com

Es Castell

Sant Joan de Binissaida.
Es Castell. Camí de Binissaida, 108.
T 971 355 598
www.binissaida.com

RURAL HOTELS AND INLAND TOURISM

Alaior

Torralbenc. Ctra. Maó-Cala en Porter, km 10. T 971 37 72 11
www.torralbenc.com

Ciutadella

Morvedrà Nou.
Camí de Sant Joan de Missa,
T 971 359 521
www.morvedranou.es

Sant Ignasi.
Crta. Cala Morell. T 971 385 575
www.santignasi.com

Tres Sants. Sant Cristòfol, 2.
T 626 053 536
www.hoteltressants.com

Es Castell

Son Granot. Ctra. Sant Felip.
T 971 35 55 55
www.songranot.com

Es Migorn Gran

Binigaus Vell. Camí de sa mala Garba, km. 0,9. T 971 054 050
www.binigausvell.com

Ferreries

Ses Sucreres Sant Joan, 15.
T 971 37 41 92
www.hotelsessucreres.com

Maó

Casa Albertí. Isabel II, 9.
T 686 393 569, www.casalberti.com

Jardí de ses Bruixes.
San Fernando, 26.
T 971 363 166
www.hotelsesbruixes.com

Sant Lluís

Alcaufar Vell.
Crta. de Sant Lluís a Alcalfar, km 8.
T 971 151 874
www.alcaufarvell.com

Biniarroca. Camí Vell 57.
T 971 150 059, www.biniarroca.com

Binissafullet Vell.
Crta. Binissafullet, 64.
T 971 150 722
www.binissafullet.com

Son Tretze. Sant Lluís. Binifadet, 20.
T 971 150 943, www.sontretze.com

CAMPING

Camping on the island is very problematic as local people have never been well-disposed to the use of their land for this purpose. It is best to use the purpose-built camp sites, book your place in advance, above all if travelling at Easter (whether they open depends on both the demand and the weather) or in the off-peak season.

Càmping S'Atalaia. Four km. from Ferreries on the Cala Galdana road. Open in the summer, just 3 km. from the beach with all kinds of services and swimming pool. Connected by bus with Ferreries and the rest of the island and also Cala Galdana.
T 971 374 232
www.campingsatalaia.com

Càmping Son Bou. Conveniently and centrally situated on the Sant Jaume road, 3.5 km. from Alaior and just 2.5 km. from the beach. As well as camping space it has bungalows and mobile homes, crazy golf, swimming pool, solarium and sports facilities in pleasant surroundings. T 971 372 727 www.campingsonbou.com

There are also some hostels situated in old watch towers or country houses, restored and adapted to take groups, and which depend on either the bishopric or local authority. Their use us usually restricted to school groups or cultural and leisure associations, but if they have free dates they can be applied for by independent groups or families. They usually have a kitchen, bathrooms and dormitories with bunk beds. The main ones are:

Alaior

Binixems, with bunk beds and basic facilities, attached to the hermitage. T 971 371 107

Santa Eularieta, with dormitories and basic facilities. T 971 365 073

Son Putxet, two equipped houses with dormitories and basic facilities. T 971 371 107

Ciutadella

Binitalaiot. With dormitories and basic facilities. T 971 383 700 www.binitalaiot.es

Es Pinaret. Well equipped hostel, and camping area. T 971 381 050

Sant Joan de Missa. Attached to the hermitage of the same name. Good facilities. T 971 380 343

Es Torretó. With dormitories and basic facilities. T 971 365 073

Sa Vinyeta. Youth host open to all ages. Good facilities. T 971 487 763

Es Mercadal

Sannctuary of El Toro. Symbolic spot, making use of the space offered by the monastic cells. T 971 375 060

Ferreries

Es Canaló. At the start of the Algendar ravine. T 971 374 072

Sant Lluís

Biniparratx campsite. With house-refuge and wild camping. T 971 364 534

Es Pinaret de s'Algar. Camping area with drinking water, tables and wooden benches. T 971 150 950 | 971 150 950

Torre Son Ganxo. Refuge for fifteen people. T 971 365 073

GASTRONOMY

We have already mentioned gin and cheese, as the most emblematic of Menorca's products, but the island has much more to offer in the way of gastronomy. *De Re Cibaria* is a classic book of Menorcan cooking and is an excellent guide for those who wish to make an in-depth discovery of the island's cuisine, whether in the form of everyday dishes or other, sometimes archaic specialities. The simple tasting of local food suffices to identify its sources: the basic ingredients available, fruit of the land or the sea, and the influence of the different successive occupations (Arab, British and French) on their preparation.

Oliaigua (literally oil and water), is a simple dish considered to be ideal for all seasons, eaten cold in summer and hot in winter. It is often served accompanied by figs. The basic ingredients are onion, garlic, green peppers and tomato cooked in a deep earthenware dish and served with fine slices of dry, white bread.

Caldereta de llagosta (lobster stew), is the island's most famous dish but was regarded, before the arrival of tourism, as simple fare which the fishermen would prepare on board their boats. Today it is considered as food fit for a king. *Calderetes* are also made with other kinds of fish and shellfish.

Arròs de la terra (Rice of the earth and similar to North African couscous) or baked aubergines are, if well prepared, as simple as they are delicious. Based on baked dough there are many recipes, such as the ***formatjades*** with cheese, to the ***coques de tomàtiga*** (tomato crêpes). Among the cooked meats feature the ***sobrassada***, ***camot*** and ***carn i xua***.

From the sea, apart from the wealth of fish caught in the surrounding waters, come es*copinyes,* sea dates, and corns. Savoury and sweet pastries include the ***formatjades*** and ***coques*** of Ciutadella, the famous ***amargos***, ***carquinyols*** and ***turró cremat*** of Mercadal and *crespells*, *pastissets* and *ensaimades* to be found everywhere and we recommend a stop-off at C'as Sucrer in Es Mercadal to try them.

Well, who could question the presence of an authentic Menorcan cuisine when the most international sauce of all is called **mahonesa**? (mayonnaise).

The next question is, of course, where can you eat well? There is so much choice in terms of restaurants and the difference in quality among them. Many of them will be trumpeted by the very tourist industry and wherever you are you will surely come across their propaganda. But by going for a "bit of adventure" can also afford some pleasant surprises: we do not disregard this alternative at all. The list below is just a small taste of what's on offer and we apologise for any omissions that are due to the lack of space.

TRADITIONAL COOKING

More and more restaurants are offering traditional dishes on their menus, some of them working hard to preserve and recover the old recipes of traditional Menorcan cuisine. We recommend these:

Ca n'Aguedet. Es Mercadal. Restaurant and tavern. Lepanto, 23.
Restaurant: T 971 375 391
Tavern: T 971 375 334

Molí des Racó. Es Mercadal. Old flour mill rehabilitated as a restaurant. Major, 53,. T 971 375 392
www.restaurantmolidesraco.com

S'Engolidor. Es Migjorn Gran. Small inn with authentic Menorca cuisine. Major, 3. T 971 370 193

FISH AND SHELLFISH

The fact that Menorca is surrounded by sea means that there are a host of fishing restaurants: there are all kinds and at all price ranges, from simple prepared fish and seafood dishes to restaurants with an extensive wine list, rice dishes and lobster stews. Many of them are near the coast and, therefore, the wonderful views are a perfect dressing to the dish chosen. We recommend the following, for their location and quality:

Ciutadella

Café Balear. Mythical restaurant in the port, it has its own boat, thus ensuring the variety and freshness of its fish dishes. Pla de Sant Joan, 15. T 971 380 005
www.cafebalear.com

Restaurante des Port. Located in a cave of the port cliff, here we can delight in all kinds of rice dishes and a fine selection of wines. Marina, 23, T 971 480 022.

Es Castell

El Trébol. Well-known restaurant with regular clientele, with excellent service and fine ingredients, it is situated in the pretty pedestrian port area of Cales Fonts, 43.
T 971 367 097
www.trebolmenorca.es

Vell Parrander. Also at Cales Fonts, 52, they specialise in lobster stew and locally-caught fish. You may be able to see them unloading the fish off the boats and, if you are lucky, listen to shanty songs in the restaurant. T 971 369 419

Ferreries

Binisues. Specialising in lobster, rice dishes and locally-caught fish. Very interesting for its traditional architecture and exhibition of antiques, farming implements and typical curiosities of rural life. In the district of Ferreries, km 31.6 of the Maó-Ciutadella road, at the turning for the Cami dels Alocs.
T 971 373 728.

Fornells

Es Cranc Pelut. On the Seafront, number 98, facing the bay of Fornells, capital of the lobster stew, it is one of the restaurants that make it the best. The seafood is excellent. Passeig Marítim, 98. T 971 376 743

Sa Llagosta. You can enjoy a good lobster stew here too, as well as fish and seafood dishes and the occasional creative cuisine dish. Gabriel Gelabert, 12. T 971 376 566

Ses Salines. In the urbanisation of the same name, with a terrace that seems to float over the sea, with modern and beautifully prepared cuisine. T 971 376 745

Maó

S'Espigó. Small family restaurant with welcoming atmosphere. Fresh fish and seafood. Moll de Llevant, 267. T 971 369 909

Es Cap Roig. Close to the beach of Sa Mesquida, and on top of the cliff, we come across this restaurant in an idyllic setting. Wide variety of fresh fish from which we can try the typical Menorcan prawn. On the right of the road, before reaching Sa Mesquida. T 971 188 383
www.restaurantcaproig.com

Can Bernat des Grau was before... in Es Grau, but in its new location keeps the marine atmosphere and excellent cuisine of fish and seafood. Road Maó-Fornells, 77.
T 650 974 685
www.canbernatdesgrau.com

TAPAS OR LIGHT SNACKS BY THE SEA

Bar Tritón. In the port of Ciutadella, it has a wide selection of tapas.
T 971 380 002

Es Bruc. With a large terrace facing the beach of Santo Tomás, in Es Migjorn Gran, and with a great view at sunset, we can taste the local meat dishes, after having had a pleasant dip in the sea.
T 971 370 488

Nou Vimpi. Another spot with good and varied tapas in the town of Ferreries. Open every day, and almost at any time. Plaça Príncep Joan Carles, 4. T 971 373 199

Ses Forquilles. In the centre of Maó, Sa Rovellada de Dalt, with creative tapas, many of them prepared on ordering.

Santa Rita Tapas Bar.
Special and creative tapas in the centre of Maó. Plaza Bastió, 14.
T 971 352 297

La Rueda. In Sant Lluís, a very popular tapas bar with the local people in the eastern area.

El Txoco. Tapas and seafaring cuisine in Binissafúller. Gregal,11.
T 971 157 395

Na Rosa. Specialising in cheese and sausage platters, pleasant spot in the small square of the Cala Torret urbanisation.
Plaça de Sa Font, 28.
T 971 150 803, www.narosa.es

RESTAURANTS WITH SPECIAL CHARM

In Menorca there are a lot of restaurants where the owner is often on the front line taking care of the smallest details. Many of them are in typical Menorcan country or village houses. They have a wide-ranging cuisine, each with their own style. They are perfect for a supper with friends and for special occasions, above all on summer nights.

Ciutadella

Cas Ferrer de sa Font. It is an old village blacksmith's. Ecological cuisine, fine Mediterranean and Menorcan cuisine, in a welcoming atmosphere. Portal de sa Font, 16. T 971 480 784, www.casferrer.com

Cas Cònsul. It is an old house remodelled in avant-garde style. Excellent views over the port. Plaça des Born, 17.
T 971 484 654
www. casconsol.com

Es Mercadal

Ca n'Olga. Good atmosphere and good food, in a typical now classic restaurant in the centre of the island. Pont de na Macarrana.
T 971 375 459

Ferreries

Liorna. A village house, exhibitions by local artists, excellent cuisine and exquisite service: this is the atmosphere of this small restaurant at Carrer de Dalt, 9.
T 971 373 912.

Maó

Aroma Sensacions. Select restaurant, one of the best views of the port from the terrace, designer and avant-garde cuisine and a wide selection of wines. Moll de Llevant, 314. T 971 363 594

Sant Climent

Es Molí de Foc. Specialising in Mediterranean cuisine and rice dishes, this restaurant in an old village house has been plying its trade for years. Sant Llorenç, 65.
T 971 153 222

Sant Lluís

Sa Pedrera des Pujol. Beautiful country house situated in the country house of Torret, 23. It is a romantic restaurant with a terrace-garden, where they revive forgotten Menorcan recipes, giving them their special touch. Extensive wine list.
T 971 150 717

La Caraba. A classic for summer suppers in an old house in S'Uestrà, 78. The cuisine is original and tasty, the ingredients carefully chosen, and the service excellent.
T 971 150 682

Sa Parereta d'en Doro. On the way to Binisafuet, number 75, we come across a typically Menorcan restaurant, with a very well prepared cuisine. T 971 150 353
www.sapareretadendoro.com

TRANSPORT

AIR

Two companies run scheduled flights throughout the year from Barcelona, Palma de Mallorca, Madrid and Valencia: **Iberia** (www.iberia.es) and **Air Europa** (www.aireuropa.com). There are more flights on offer at Easter and in the summer, when several airlines run flights between the island and distinct European capitals. For example: **Vueling** (www.vueling.com) and **Ryanair** (www.ryanair.com). The airport is situated on the Me-14 road, between Maó and Sant Climent. T 971 157 000, www.aena.es.

BOAT

In winter the **Acciona-Trasmediterránea** company runs a service between Maó and Barcelona with three trips per week. This route becomes daily at Easter and during the summer months, and is often backed up by a second boat during peak holiday periods. There are two types of boat: a fast one, covering the trip in four hours, and another one that does it in eight hours. Another regular route is Maó-Palma (about six hours journey), which continues on to Valencia, with a weekly service throughout the year.
T 902 454 645
www.trasmediterranea.es

Baleària undertakes, throughout the year, daily trips to Barcelona, as well as covering the route to Mallorca (Ciutadella-Alcúdia).
T 902 160 180, www.balearia.com

BUSES

There are three companies that run regular bus routes:

Transports Menorca S.A. Cover the Maó–Ciutadella, Maó–Es Castell, Maó–Sant Lluís, Maó–Es Migjorn Gran–Ferreries, Maó–Sant Climent routes, and those round the urbanisations in the southeast area. The bus station in Maó is in S'Esplanada.
T 971 360 475, www.tmsa.es

Autos Fornells S.A. Link Maó with Fornells and the urbanised beaches on the northeast coast (Arenal d'en Castell, Son Parc, Platges de Fornells and Es Grau).
T 971 154 390 | 686 939 246
www.autosfornells.com

Autocars Torres. Links Ciutadella with the urbanised beaches around the city (Sa Caleta, Santandria, Cala Blanca, Cala en Bosc, Son Xoriguer, Cala en Blanes, Los Delfines and Cala en Forcat). It also connects Maó with its port and the airport.
T 971 386 461, www.e-torres.net

We recommend you check the timetables in advance at the bus stations or in the tourist information offices since in winter the service is greatly reduced. You can also check the website www.menorca.tib.org where you will find all the up-to-date timetables.

CAR

There are international and local car hire firms in most of the towns. The biggest ones have offices and pick-up and return services at the airport. Remember that the demand increases greatly during the peak holiday season and it is a good idea to book your vehicle in advance. Travel agencies and airlines often provide plane-car and boat-car packages that are more economical.

You can also hire motorbikes, mopeds and bicycles (even tandems) at many places.

Regarding the traffic regulations, you should remember that the speed limit on roads between towns is 90 kph and in the towns 40 kph; and on the rural tracks it is a good idea, as well as showing greater prudence, to use your horn and lights on many of the bends where there is poor visibility. The lack of special lanes for bicycles or mopeds, and the wide pavements for pedestrians, is another factor that makes it recommendable to drive slowly, also because of the frequency of brows of hills. Finally, remember the international motto, "If you drink, don't drive": you will be fined if a breath test gives a result of over 0.3 g/l.

MEDICAL SERVICES

The main public health centre (www.portaldesalut.caib.es) is the **Hospital Mateu Orfila**, in Ronda de Malbúger, 1, Maó. T 971 487 000, www.ibsalut.es

For **emergencies** you should call **061**.

Each area of the island has its own Health Centre. The centre for the eastern area, **Dalt Sant Joan**, is in Maó, at c/ Fornells 107-109, T 971 353 255.

That of the centre, **Es Banyer**, is in Alaior, Carrer Mestre Duràn s/n, T 971 372 931.

And the one for the west, **Canal Salat**, in Ciutadella, is at Carrer St. Antoni Mª Claret s/n, T 971 480 111/971 480 112. Each town also has a Basic Health Unit, where less serious health problems can be dealt with.

In Maó, in Dalt Sant Joan, there is a Women's Medical Attention Service. T 971 356 942

As regards private clinics, in Ciutadella there is the **Clínica Juaneda Menorca** (T 971 480 505), C/ Canonge Moll, s/n, and in Maó, the **Policlínica Verge de Gràcia** (T 971 351 115), c/ Vives Llull, 6.

The Red Cross also has assistance centres on the main beaches.

AMBULANCES

Emergencies:
Mobile ICU.................... T 061
Red Cross:
Maó............... T 971 361 180
Ciutadella .... T 971 381 993
Alaior.............. T 971 371 238
Ferreries........... T 971 373 139
Mercadal.......... T 971 375 300
Sant Lluís...........T 971 151 001

TELEPHONE NUMBERS OF INTEREST

Menorca Island Council
.................T 971 356 050
www.cime.es
Tourism:
Fundació Foment del turisme
Menorca........... T 971 368 678
www.menorca.es
Tourist information offices:
Maó............... T 971 367 415
Ciutadella .... T 971 382 693
Aeroport .... T 971 157 115
Puerto de Maó .... T 971 355 952
Fornells.............T 971 376 437
Councils:
Alaior.............. T 971 371 002
www.alaior.org
Ciutadella .... T 971 381 050
www.ajciutadella.org
Es Castell.......... T 971 365 193
www.aj-escastell.org
Es Mercadal .... T 971 375 002
www.aj-esmercadal.org
Es Migjorn Gran ... T 971 370 110
www.ajmigjorngran.org
Ferreries........... T 971 373 003
www.ajferreries.org
Maó............... T 971 369 800
www.ajmao.org
Sant Lluís.......... T 971 150 950
www.ajsantlluis.org
Emergencies: .... T 112
Police:
National Police .... T 091
Guàrdia Civil................ T 062
Maó Local Police .... T 092 .
.....................T 971 363 961
Ciutadella Local Police...... T 092 .
.....................T 971 380 787
Fire brigade:
Maó................T 971 351 011
Ciutadella .... T 971 380 809
Radio Taxi.........T 971 367 111
Consulates:
Great Britain....... T 971 367 818
Germany .... T 971 361 668
France..............T 971 354 387
Italy .... T 971 724 214
Netherlands .... T 971 354 363